Hand Carving Snowmen and Santas

By

Mike Shipley

Fox
Chapel Publishing Co. Inc.

Rochester Public Library

Hand Carving Snowmen and Santas, Copyright © 2000, Fox Chapel Publishing Company Inc.

The patterns contained herein are copyrighted by the author. Artists may make three copies of these patterns for personal use and may make any number of projects based on these patterns. The patterns themselves, however, are not to be duplicated for resale or distribution under any circumstances. Any such copying is a violation of copyright laws.

Publisher: Alan Giagnocavo
Project Editor: Ayleen Stellhorn
Desktop Specialist: Linda L. Eberly, Eberly Designs Inc.
Interior Photography: Bob Fleming, Fleming Foto
Cover Photography: Carl Shuman, Owl Hill Studios

ISBN# 1–56523–129–5

To order your copy of this book
please send check or money order
for the cover price plus $3.00 shipping to:
Fox Books
1970 Broad Street
East Petersburg, PA 17520

Or visit us on the web at
www.carvingworld.com

Manufactured in Korea

ACKNOWLEDGMENTS

Thanks to Sherry and the girls for living with all of my long hours in the shop. Thanks to Bob Fleming at Fleming Foto.

Table of Contents

Introduction iv
Chapter One – Tools and Techniques 1
Chapter Two – Grinning Snowman 4
    Ready-to-Use Pattern 6
    Step-by-Step Carving 7
    Step-by-Step Painting 12
Chapter Three – Santa's Surprise 14
    Ready-to-Use Pattern 16
    Step-by-Step Carving 17
    Step-by-Step Painting 27
Chapter Four – Patterns 30
    Snowman in a Top Hat 30
    Snowlady 32
    Cowboy Snowman 34
    Snowman and Santa Spoons 36
    Traditional Santa 38
    Uncle Sam Santa 40
    Old World Santa 42
    Saint Nicholas 44
    Woodland Santa 46
    Mrs. Claus 48
    Mr. Claus 50
    Cowboy Santa 52
Afterword 54

INTRODUCTION

While putting this book together I found myself trying to come up with a simple, witty definition of this "sickness" called woodcarving. After many years of production carving and hundreds—no make that several thousand—characters, I still can't wait to finish one piece so that I can start another one. No doubt we are all afflicted in different ways, but the thrill of a finished piece with the opportunity to do better on the next one is about the only definition that I can come up with.

As you can see, the theme of this book is snowmen and Santas. At one time or another, we've all envisioned the "real" Santa Claus. That's what I had in mind when I assembled the Santa projects for this book. Of course, I couldn't include all the versions of Santa Claus, but there are enough ideas here to keep you busy for a while—plus a few snowmen for a change of pace.

In the first section of this book, you'll find instructions for carving and painting the "Grinning Snowman." This short little fellow is a typical, well-rounded man of snow, complete with a hat and scarf. The second section of this book shows you how to carve and paint a Santa piece that I've named "Santa's Surprise." This Santa is ready to deliver a sack full of toys to some very lucky girls and boys. The last section of this book is filled with patterns. Use these as they are presented here or alter them to suit your own needs.

I always apply the same two rules to every piece I carve: 1) Add enough detail to make it interesting. 2) Keep it simple enough to make it fun. Try following these rules as you carve the projects in this book.

Mike Shipley
c/o Fox Chapel Publishing
1970 Broad Street
East Petersburg, PA 17520
editors@carvingworld.com

CHAPTER ONE

Tools and Techniques

Carving snowmen and santas is a great way to enjoy the holiday season. Snowmen capture all the fun of winter and tap into the child in all of us. Santas, with their jolly faces and usually over-stuffed stomachs, have grown to embody not only the spirit of Christmas, but the entire idea behind the joy of giving.

But even more importantly, carving snowmen and santas can provide a much-needed break from more complicated projects. The projects in this book are simple enough that they can help you "take a breather" from a frustrating project or relax from a hard day at the office. Working on a snowman or a santa —anytime of the year—can be great fun.

This chapter includes everything you need to know to get started on the two projects in this book. We'll take a look at the tools I use for carving snowmen and santas, and review some specific carving and painting techniques.

Tools

A variety of gouges and knives are used in the following projects. The specific tool sizes are mentioned in the carving steps.

I used hand tools for the projects in this book. Those pictured above are the hand tools I commonly use. You do not have to purchase all of these tools to complete the projects in this book. At the very least, you'll need a carving knife and a v-tool.

When I carve, I use a knife and a v-tool more than anything else. You can get a lot of work done with a v-tool. A good example of this is step #10 in the Santa project. I use the sides of the v-tool like I would use a knife blade.

I have certain tools that I use for certain jobs. For instance, for carving eyes I use a very fine detail knife that I don't use for anything else. Again, these tools are optional. They do make the carving go quicker and easier, but the same results can be achieved with common tools and a little extra effort.

As a general rule, I always use the largest tool possible. This allows me to make fewer cuts, which in turn, speeds up my carving time.

Sharpening

As any carver knows, sharp tools are a must. I use a belt sander with a one-inch-wide, fine-grit belt to shape the blade. I follow this with a cotton buffing wheel dressed with jewelers rouge compound.

I also use a fine grinding wheel mounted on an ordinary bench grinder. This method gives me a sharp edge in a hurry, but it does take practice. Over-heating the blade is always the problem and must be avoided. An over-heated blade will lose its ability to hold an edge and could become brittle.

Sharpening requires practice and patience. Just work on it until you find a method that fits your needs. Once you get a good edge established, buffing will keep it in good shape.

If you don't feel comfortable with the more aggressive methods I've just mentioned, you can always use whetstones followed with a leather strop. Although a stone is much slower, it's also hard to go wrong with a good stone and a strop. I used this method for many years until I became more confident with a grinder.

With any bench knife, I always shape the blade to remove any bevel on the edge. I want the knife blade to come down to the cutting edge in a wedge shape. The blade will cut more easily with the bevel removed.

Carving Snowmen and Santas — Chapter One

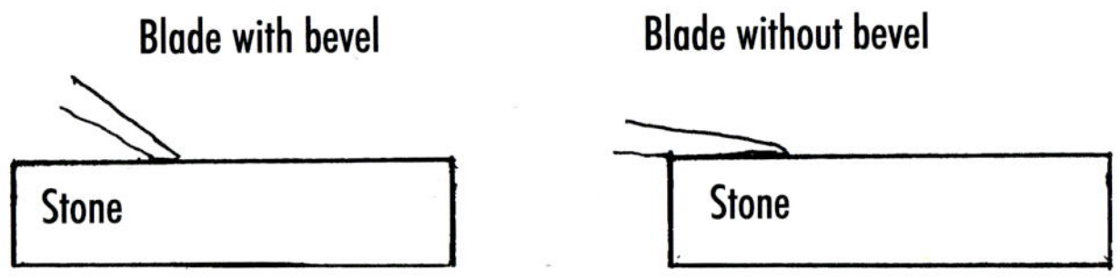

TOOLS AND TECHNIQUES

Notice in the illustration, the blade without the bevel will lie flat on the sharpening stone. When I remove the bevel on a blade, I use a stone to avoid overheating the metal. Lay the blade flat on the stone. As you move the blade on the stone, use a push-pull motion, instead of just one stroke. Actually, you will be stroking the blade back and forth as you move the blade across the stone edge first. These back and forth strokes will speed up the sharpening process. Keep checking the edge and you can see the bevel start to disappear. When the bevel is gone, buff the edge with a buffing wheel.

Buffing the edge of the blade as needed will keep the knife cutting cleanly. After the blade is buffed several times, a worn bevel will form on the edge again. Repeat the steps above to bring back a good, flat edge.

Carving can be tiring; a beveled edge adds to the force that must be applied to move the edge through the wood. A beveled edge is less aggressive, but it will cause you to work harder. This principle also applies to gouges and v-tools.

Carving Tips

One carving tip I always like to mention is the use of what I call carving stops. There are three types of stops. One is a cut made to stop the blade from cutting any farther. Another is a natural stop, such as removing wood on Santa's coat up to the beard. In that case, the beard acts as the stop.

The third and most important carving stop—and the one that I always stress—is the thumb on the hand opposite your carving hand. I carve with my right hand, so that would be my left thumb. Whether you are pushing or pulling on the blade, use that thumb to apply pressure to control or stop the blade. A carving stop will prevent an unwanted cut on your carving or, worse yet, on your finger.

Carving also requires good lighting, especially if your eyes

A knife cut along the hairline acts as a stop cut. Stop cuts will help you control the amount of wood you remove from various areas on the carving.

The thumb of the hand opposite your carving hand is perhaps the most important carving stop. Apply pressure with this thumb to control or stop the blade.

are not what they used to be. I use a fluorescent shop light directly over my workbench. It provides a sharp, clear light and helps to control shadows.

Painting Tips

There are so many painting and finishing methods used on woodcarvings today that it would take volumes to mention them all. I've tried just about every method I could think of, and many of them worked well. Unfortunately, most are time consuming and complicated.

Painting and finishing should be fun. If painting becomes a time-consuming and complicated procedure, then it's not very fun. Remember the two rules that I mentioned in the introduction: 1) Add just enough detail to make it interesting, and 2) keep it simple enough to make it fun. These rules apply to painting as well.

I like to use the inexpensive acrylic paints in the squeeze bottles. I use them because they're so versatile. I just thin the paint with water until I get the shade I want. These paints also

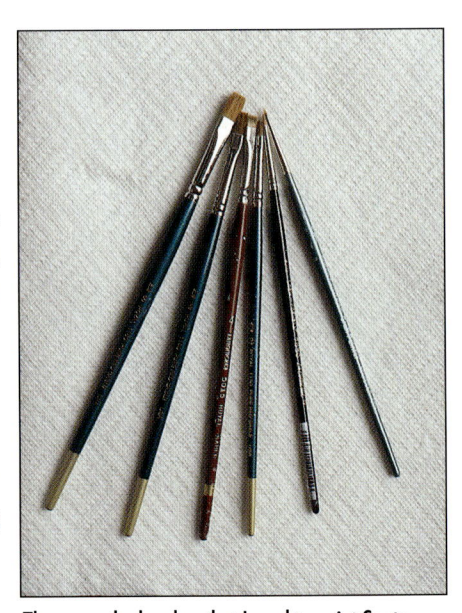

These are the brushes that I used to paint Santa (left to right): 4/0 spotter, #2 shader, #4 shader, #4 short blender and #8 shader.

dry in just a few minutes, which allows me to continue painting without a break between colors. The only problem with these acrylics is that when they dry, they have a harsh look. I always apply stain after the paint dries completely to give the colors a softer look.

Although I use the more inexpensive paint, I always use good quality sable brushes. They seem to last longer than the synthetic brushes. Always clean your brushes well after each use and they'll last even longer.

I mentioned earlier to always use the largest tool possible when carving. That is not the case when you paint a carving. I use a number of different brushes in a variety of sizes. The rule of thumb is to use whatever size brush is necessary to avoid over-painting or bleeding into another color.

Painting stops, which are similar to the carving stops described earlier, help to control the paint brush just as you would control a knife blade. You'll notice in the painting steps how I plant my little finger to steady my hand and control the brush.

Be sure to take your time when painting. If the colors overlap or bleed into each other, it usually can't be corrected. With any colors, especially the darker, harsher ones, I use circular blending strokes to blend the paint on the surface of the wood to get good, even coverage.

Staining

I use boiled linseed oil with a very small amount of raw umber oil paint from a squeeze tube. Fill a large-mouth 28-oz. plastic peanut butter jar almost to the top with linseed oil. Then squeeze about one inch of paint into the oil. Shake the container vigorously to mix the stain. The stain will separate, so be sure to mix it again if you allow it to sit for any length of time between uses.

There are two ways to apply the stain to your piece. Either brush the stain on the piece or dip the piece into the container. I always dip the smaller pieces. Of course, larger pieces will have to be brushed. Allow the excess to drip off, then towel the piece dry with paper towels.

Do not store the stain-soaked towels. Linseed oil will combust, I know that from experience. Immediately after staining, incinerate the towels or store them in a container approved for flammable materials.

CHAPTER TWO

Grinning Snowman

Snowmen are easy to carve because of their basic shape. We'll carve my version in this chapter, but this little guy is designed to be versatile. Use your imagination and you can carve several different snowmen from this same pattern.

Snowmen are also fun to carve. If you're working on a difficult piece and you seem to run into problems with it, just lay it down for a while and carve this little guy. You'll be surprised how he'll pick up your carving spirits. This is a tactic I've used for many years. I always have a quick, easy piece to fall back on to relieve the frustration of working on a more difficult piece.

A snowman, or other simple piece, is also a great way to pick yourself up after a long day at work. If you do a lot of carving, pick-me-up pieces are very important. For me, it's snowmen. With you it might be a different subject. The point is to find your own pick-me-up piece that makes you feel good, no matter how many times you carve it. Maybe this snowman will be just the one.

You will need a basswood block measuring 2 3/8 in. wide by 2 3/8 in. thick by 4 in. long. The grain should run with the length of the block.

Materials List: Carving
basswood block 2 3/8" x 4" x 2 3/8"
pencil
heavy paper
band saw
carving glove
gouges
v-tools
carving knife
220-grit sandpaper

Materials List: Painting
spotter brush
#2 shader
#4 shader
white
tangerine orange
cadmium red medium
hunter green
black

SNOWMAN STEP-BY-STEP

In this project, we'll carve the simple version pictured here. Later, you might carve your own version. Start making your own creation by adding a bow tie or maybe a pipe in his mouth. (Height: 3 1/2")

Carving Snowmen and Santas

Chapter Two

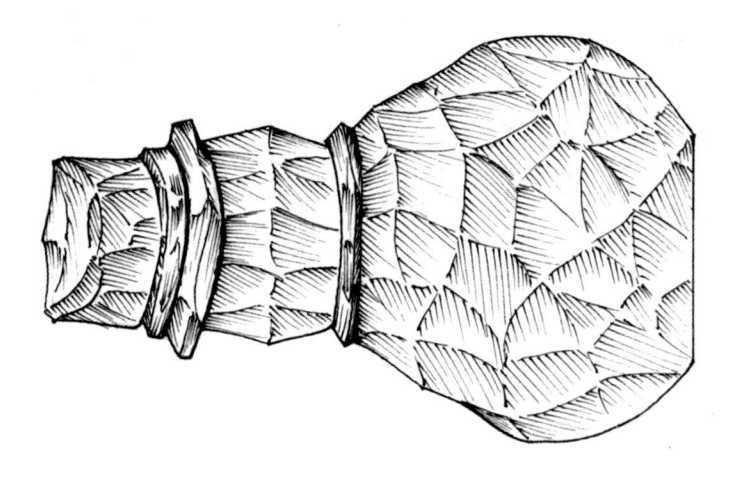

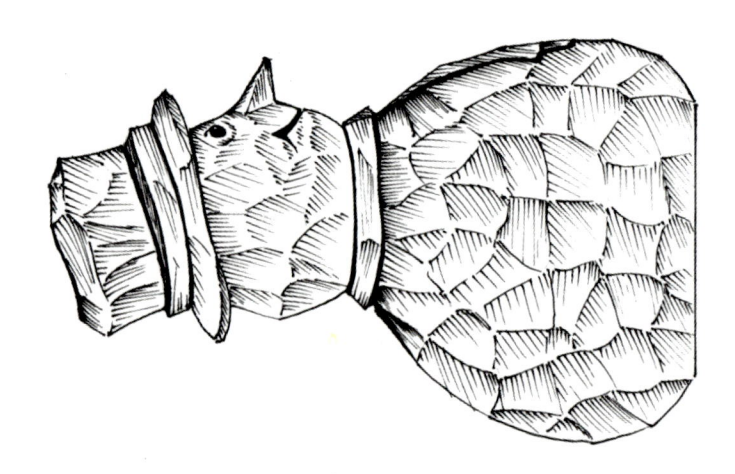

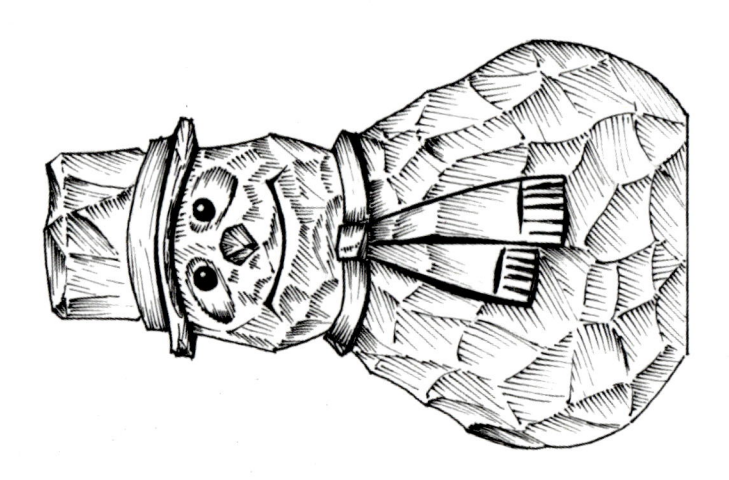

SNOWMAN STEP-BY-STEP

Chapter Two

© Mike Shipley

Carving Snowmen and Santas

SNOWMAN STEP-BY-STEP

1 First saw the side view with the band saw. Notice the hat brim on the back. To stabilize the blank on the saw table, leave extra wood on the hat brim that extends out level with the back of the snowman. That extra wood will be removed after the front view is cut. Anything to stabilize the blank is a must.

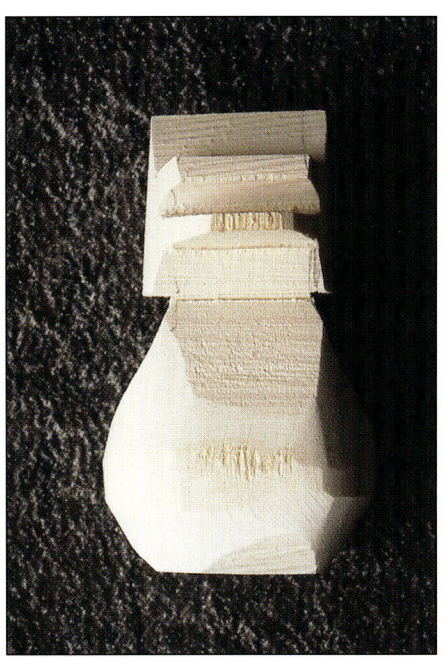

2 Now saw the front view. You'll notice I used the disc sander to remove excess wood and to help round all the edges. Keep in mind you don't see very many square snowmen.

3 Use a wide shallow gouge to start rounding the piece. A bench knife also works well in place of a gouge. The body is round so the grain will change directions. Work in the direction that the grain dictates.

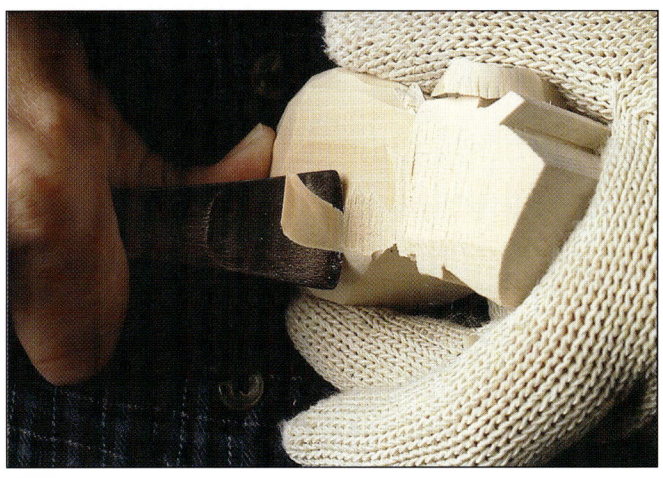

4 After moving up the body, the grain has changed direction. Just change your cutting direction and go with the grain. Notice I have my thumb set for a stop. I can also use the hat brim for a stop.

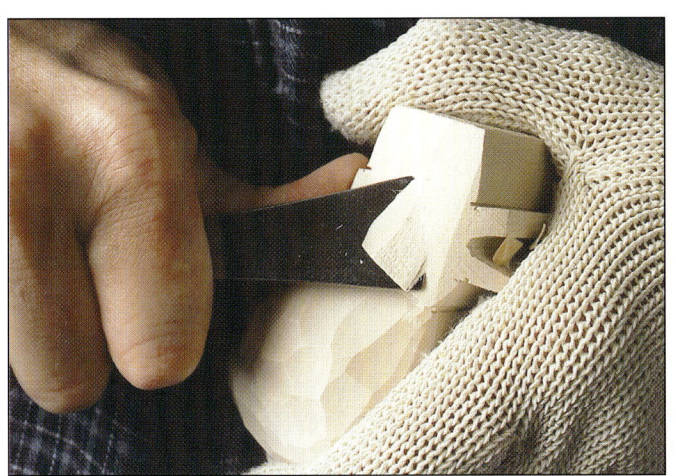

5 After the body is rounded, use the same shallow gouge to round the hat. When finished, the hat brim will extend out approximately 1/4 in. beyond the head.

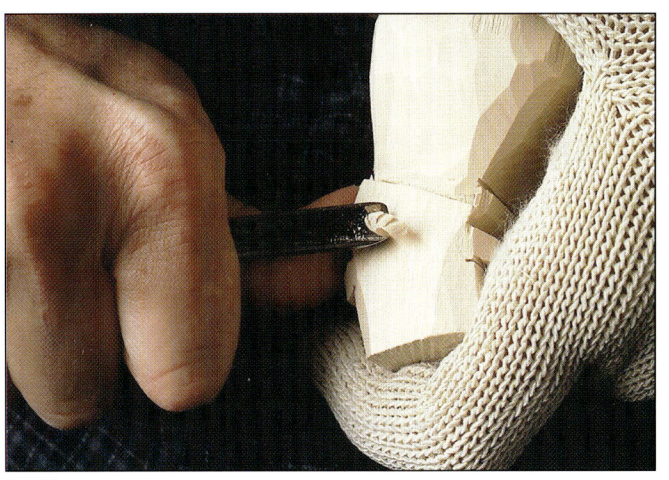

6 Use a 6mm v-tool to cut a line all the way around under the hat brim. You already have a guide to go by in the front and back. Deepen this cut to bring out the hat brim.

Carving Snowmen and Santas — Chapter Two

SNOWMAN STEP-BY-STEP

7 With the knife, clean up the head up to the hat. Round the head until the head flows cleanly up to the hat brim. Notice the stops used here.

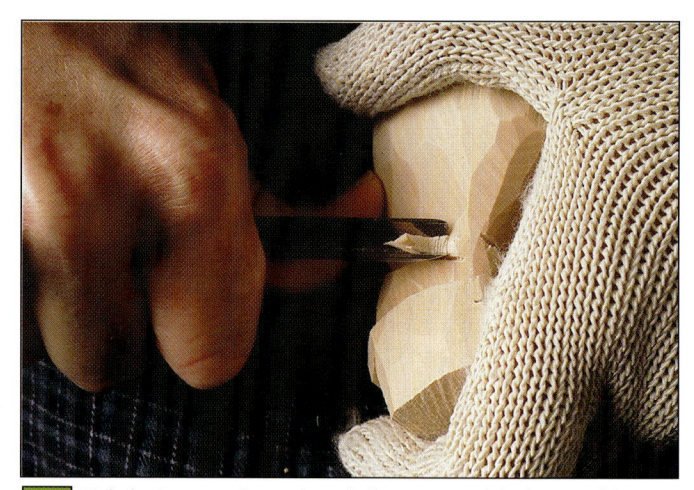

8 With the 6mm v-tool, cut a line all the way around the bottom of the head. This will be where the bottom of the head meets the scarf.

9 With the knife, round the head down to this cut. Clean up the head and body so they meet with this clean line.

10 Here you can see the clean line where the head and body meet. Now start rounding the hat down to a realistic size. There will be quite a bit of wood to remove. Here I'm using what you might call a reverse stop.

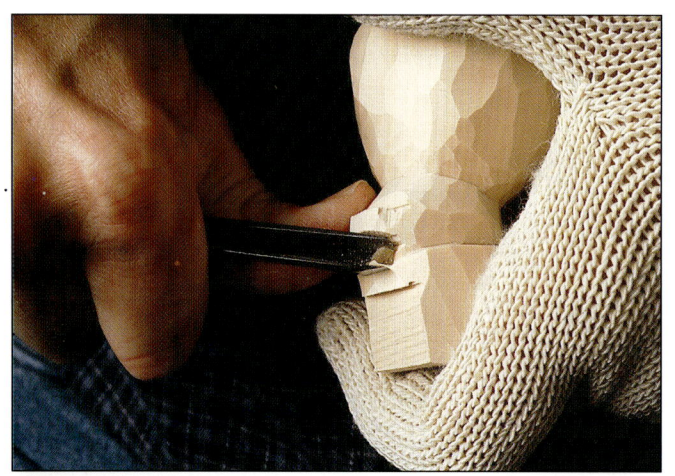

11 With the 4mm v-tool, cut up under the hat brim above the nose to dip the hat brim up over the face. Take care not to cut too deeply into the face; all you want to do is raise the hat brim.

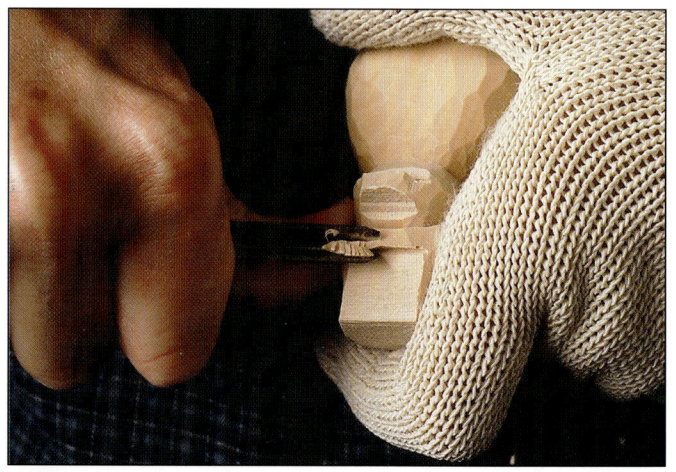

12 With the 6mm v-tool, cut around the hat to form the hat brim. Deepen this cut to bring out the brim and to lessen the size of the hat.

Chapter Two — 8 — *Carving Snowmen and Santas*

SNOWMAN STEP-BY-STEP

13 Now that the brim is formed, work the hat down until it looks natural when compared to the size of the head.

14 We'll leave the hat for a minute to pencil in the scarf. The scarf will come down the front in two different lengths and will wrap around the body at the base of the head.

15 The reason we left the hat to pencil in the scarf is so we can do two jobs while we're using the v-tool. With the 4mm v-tool, cut a line around the hat to form the hat band. The width of the band is not critical.

16 With the same v-tool, cut the scarf lines.

17 These lines outline the scarf.

18 With an 8 mm v-tool, remove wood next to the scarf to raise the scarf off the body. You can also see the hat band line. The width of the band can vary.

Carving Snowmen and Santas — Chapter Two

SNOWMAN STEP-BY-STEP

19 Now that the scarf is raised off the body, cut the fringe on the ends of the scarf with the 4mm v-tool.

20 With the knife, clean up and finish the hat above the hat band. Then finish the top of the hat.

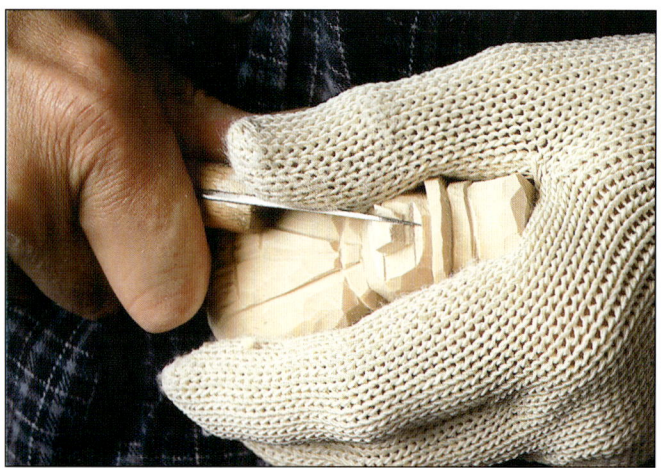

21 While you're using the knife, it's time to make the carrot nose. You might want to pencil in a centerline to center the nose on the head. Now make straight-in cuts on each side of the center. The nose will start with a triangle shape that is wider at the bottom and narrow at the top.

22 Now, carefully work the nose down to size. Remember it's a carrot nose, so it will simply be wider at the face and then come out to a point. This pointy nose is fragile now so be careful. Clean up the face area also.

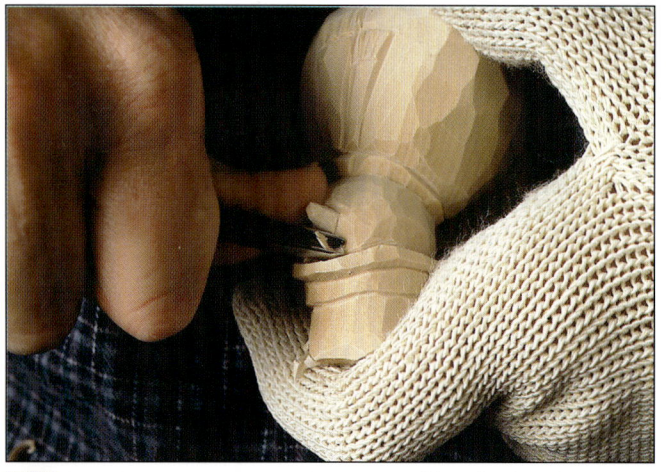

23 Use a 3mm veining gouge to scoop out wood from the eye sockets. Form the eye sockets into an oval shape.

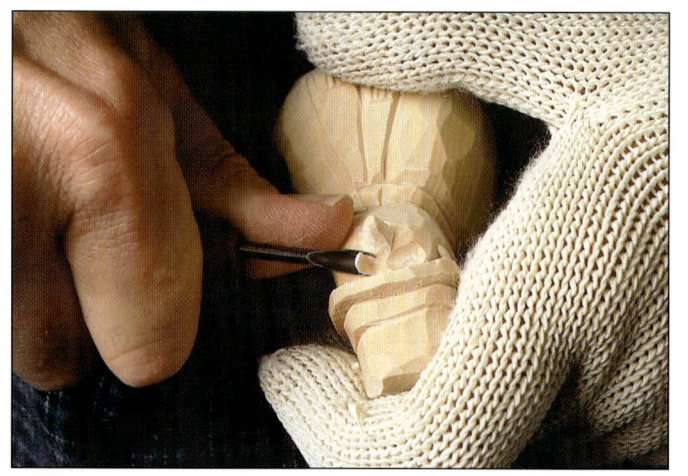

24 Clean up both sockets until the sizes and shapes match. The overall size of the sockets isn't critical, as long as they match. Try to drop the sockets down toward the outside edges of the face. This will give the eyes and face a little character.

Chapter Two — Carving Snowmen and Santas

SNOWMAN STEP-BY-STEP

25 Here you can see how the eye sockets droop in an oval shape. With the knife tip, cut a smiling half-moon-shaped mouth. Just cut a line, then trim the lower edge of this cut to slightly open the mouth.

26 With the knife, make small down cuts at each corner of the mouth. Trim the mouth into these cuts to tuck the mouth in at the corners.

27 Notice here how the mouth has the appearance of tucking in at the corners.

28 You're almost done. Take some time to sign your piece. Lucky carvers have short names, if you see what I mean.

29 With 220-grit sandpaper lightly sand the whole piece. Be careful with the nose; it is prone to breaking. Just a light sanding is all you need.

30 Your snowman is finished and ready to paint. Notice the worn look that the sanding gives. The paint and stain will enhance this look even more. If you don't prefer this look, just omit the sanding step.

Carving Snowmen and Santas · 11 · Chapter Two

SNOWMAN STEP-BY-STEP PAINTING

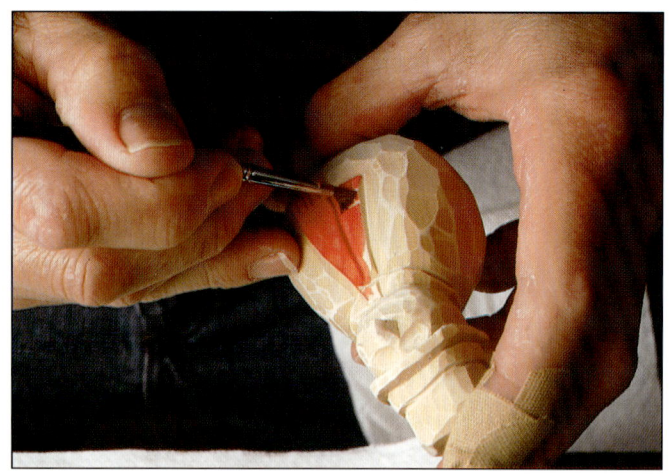

1 Use a #2 shader brush to paint the scarf and the hat band cadmium red medium.

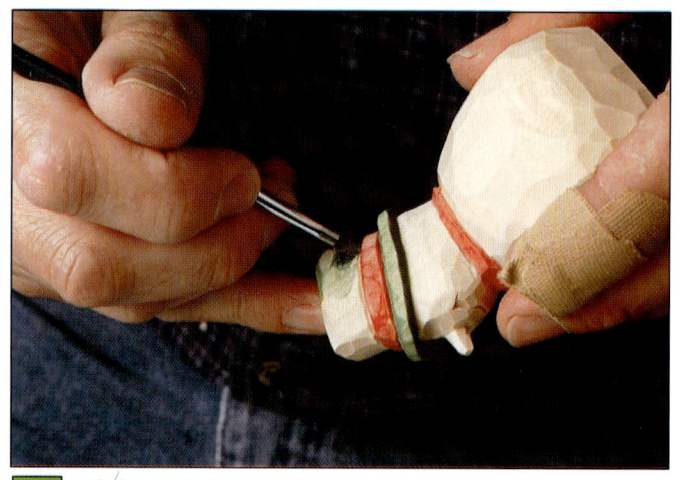

2 With the #2 shader, paint the hat hunter green.

3 With the spotter brush, paint the carrot nose tangerine orange.

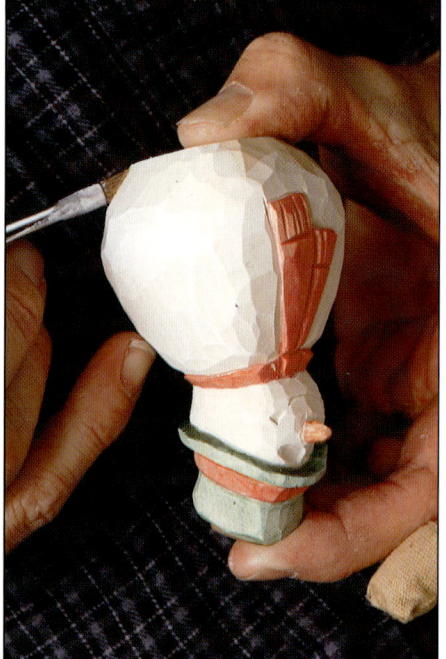

4 There are not many colors involved in painting the snowman. Once the nose, hat and scarf are done, you're ready for the white. Of course, a snowman should be a nice white, so I mix the white a little stronger. Be careful not to mix the white too strong though. You don't want a solid, painted look. I never mix acrylics so strong that they appear "painted on." I always prefer a washed look. Use a #2 shader on the head, and a #4 shader on the body. You will have a lot of wet surfaces here, so be careful not to touch the white on the other colors. Use circular blending strokes to get good, even coverage on the large body.

5 The eyes are simple. All you need is a toothpick. Cut the end off the toothpick so that it is flat and blunt. Using black paint straight from the bottle, load the flat end of the toothpick with black paint. Just touch a round eye into each eye socket. Carefully retouch the eyes to make them match, if needed.

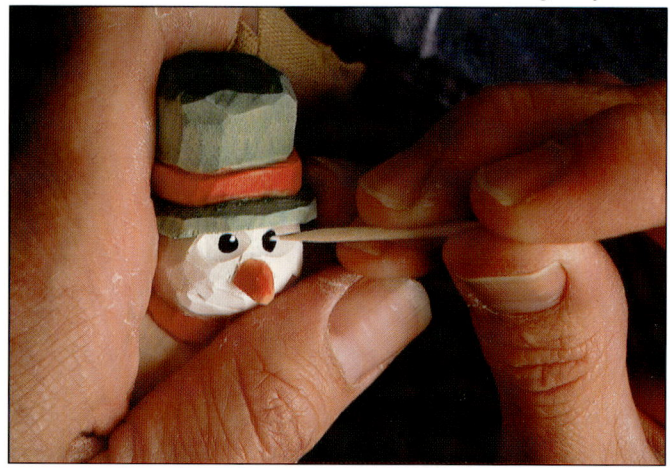

6 Let the eye dry for approximately five minutes. Use the sharp end of the toothpick and white straight from the bottle to make a small dot on the black of the eye. Notice how this highlights the eye. Let the paint dry for about one hour before staining the piece.

Chapter Two — Carving Snowmen and Santas

SNOWMAN STEP-BY-STEP

7 Staining the snowman follows the same methods outlined in chapter one. Just dip half of the snowman in the stain and let the excess stain drip off.

8 Now dip the other half of the snowman and let the excess stain drip off for a minute. Towel the surface dry with paper towels. The surface may feel a little oily when you are finished—just towel-dry it as dry as possible without rubbing too hard. Be careful with the nose while you are drying the piece because it can be easily damaged. The snowman will dry completely in about 24 hours.

9 Your finished quick-and-easy snowman is ready to enjoy.

Carving Snowmen and Santas   13   Chapter Two

CHAPTER THREE

Santa's Surprise

I designed this Santa from several versions that I have carved through the years. On a difficulty-of-carving scale, he's about a medium. One hand is in his pocket to make it easier. The other hand is holding the sack to make it more challenging. You might want to move the sack to be sitting at his feet or remove it completely to really simplify the piece. There are several possibilities, but in this case, we'll carve the version at hand.

To carve the Santa in this chapter, you will need a basswood block measuring 2 1/2 in. wide by 2 1/2 in. thick by 6 1/2 in. long. The grain should run the length of the block. I don't have a duplicating lathe, so I use a disc sander with a coarse grit disc to round the edges and remove as much excess wood as possible before I start carving.

Materials List: Carving

basswood block 2 1/2" x 6 1/2" x 2 1/2"
pencil
heavy paper
band saw
carving glove
gouges
v-tools
carving knife
220-grit sandpaper

Materials List: Painting

spotter brush
#2 shader
#4 shader
#6 shader
#8 shader
#4 blender
white
flesh color
thicket green
licorice black
cadmium red medium
hunter green
coffee bean brown

SANTA STEP-BY-STEP

This traditional Santa has one hand in his pocket to make the carving easier. To make the project even easier, carve his sack at his feet or remove it completely. (Height: 6")

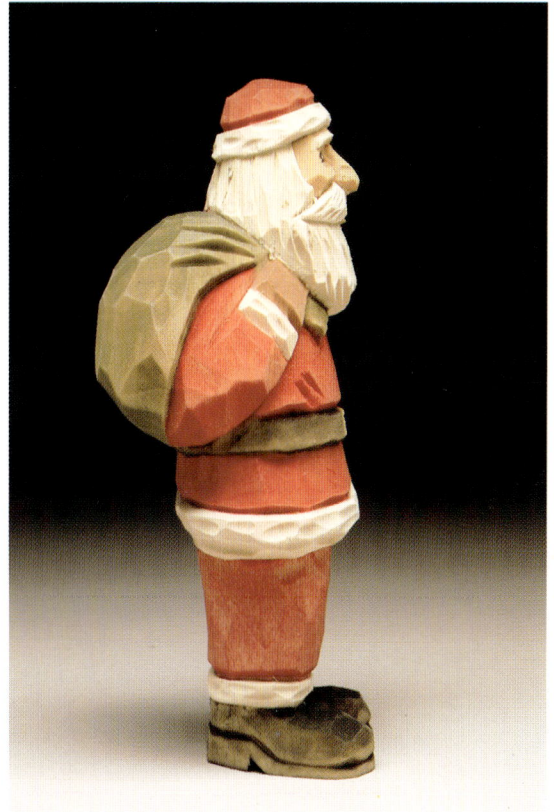

Carving Snowmen and Santas

Chapter Three

SANTA STEP-BY-STEP

Enlarge 117%

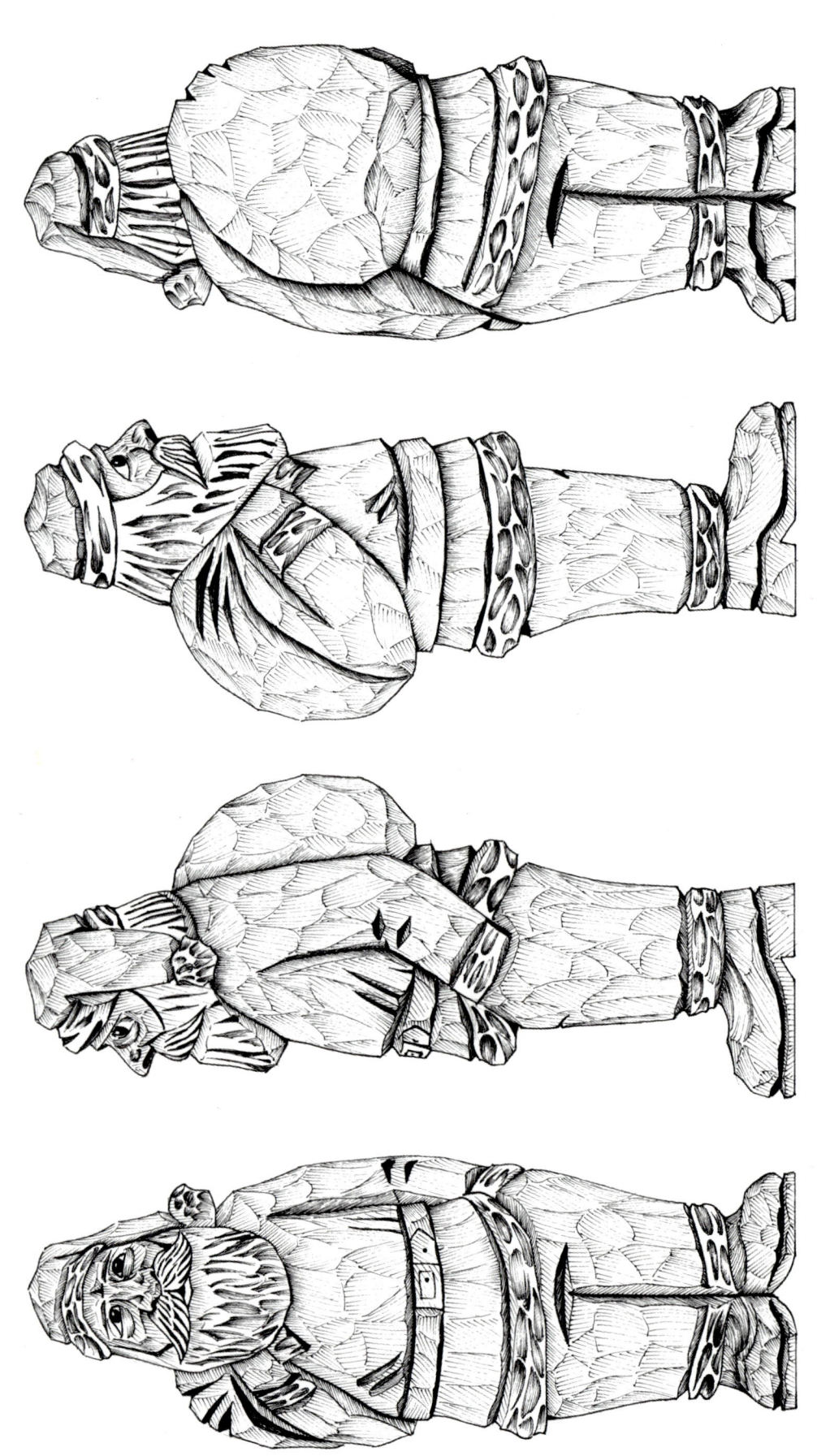

© Mike Shipley

Chapter Three — Carving Snowmen and Santas

SANTA STEP-BY-STEP

1 Transfer the pattern from this book to a thicker piece of paper, then cut it out. This will give you a reusable pattern and keep your book intact. Place the side view pattern on the block and trace around it with a pencil. Cut as close to the lines as possible with a band saw. Always cut the side view first. Usually, more distinctive features can be seen from the side so it helps to cut the side view first. Take your time and remove as much waste wood as possible. Leave wood attached to the back of the head and feet to help stabilize the block on the saw table.

2 Trace the front view on to the block and saw as close to the lines as possible. Now you can see the benefit of leaving the extra wood on the back of the head and feet. An unstable block on a saw table is dangerous—remember you'll need those fingers when you start carving.

3 For years I carved without a carving glove and paid the price with more cuts than I care to remember. Now, I use a cut-resistant glove or a good quality leather glove. The leather glove is more comfortable, but of course, it doesn't resist cuts. Start carving by rounding the blank with a wide shallow gouge to round the edges and remove some excess wood. A bench knife will work well if you don't have a wide shallow gouge.

4 Notice the large cuts that were made with the wide shallow gouge. Now use a 12mm v-tool to make deep cuts on each side of the tassel. These cuts will raise the tassel off the hat. Just roughly shape the tassel for now, making the ball or lower end narrower than the top, which will blend into the hat.

5 Use a pencil to mark the sack lines. The sack lies on the back of the arm and will come up to the back of the head. Remember that the sack will be rounded on all edges and will be pulled over across the back to the right hand.

6 Next pencil in the beard and hairline around the shoulders. The beard length in front was cut with the band saw. This gives me a guideline for how long the beard will be.

Carving Snowmen and Santas — **Chapter Three**

SANTA STEP-BY-STEP

7 With a large v-tool, cut the pencil line around the beard and the hair line. Use a bench knife to shape the head and the shoulder area. Use the cut made by the v-tool as a carving stop between the hair and the shoulders.

8 As you can see, the head is now rounded to a more realistic size. Pencil in the arm lines and the lines for the sack. The end of the sack will be tucked under the mitten. Remember that the sack lies on the back of the arm.

9 Cut around the sack line to separate the sack from the back of the arm. Pencil in the other arm line. Santa's hand will be in his pocket, so just bring the line for the arm down to the pants.

10 With a 12mm v-tool, cut the arm lines and deepen these cuts to bring out the arms. In an area like this, use the sides of the v-tool as if it were a knife. This sometimes saves reaching for another tool.

11 Now use the knife to clean up and shape the arm down to a finished size. Remember earlier I mentioned carving stops? Here's a good example of how to use the opposite thumb to control the blade.

12 Use the knife to clean up the other arm. Also clean up the coat area up to the arm. Shape the coat area to a good size and shape. Round any square areas. The coat should appear rounded and flow with the shape of the body.

Chapter Three — Carving Snowmen and Santas

SANTA STEP-BY-STEP

13 On this arm, use an 8mm v-tool to cut a line down to the bend of the arm. Then cut a line to separate the sack and the arm. The sack lies on the back of the arm. Notice the end of the sack extends out from under the hand or mitten.

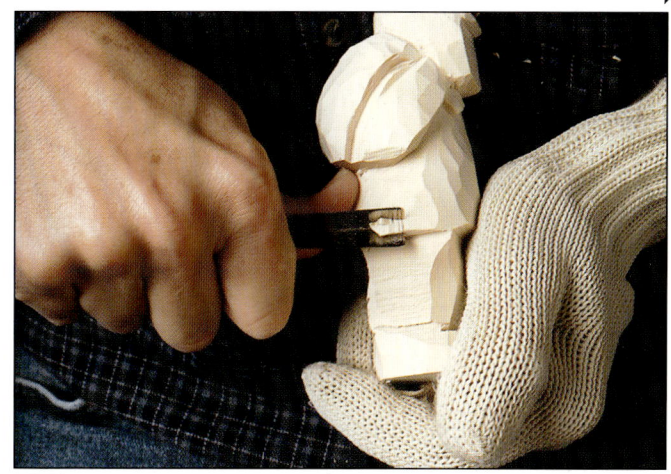

14 With a large v-tool cut around the bottom of the coat hem. The hem will be lower at this point and will then sweep up to be tucked under the arm where the hand enters the pocket.

15 Deepen the cut around the coat hem to raise the coat off the pants. Use the sides of the v-tool to help clean up this area. Also use the large v-tool to clean up the coat up to the sack.

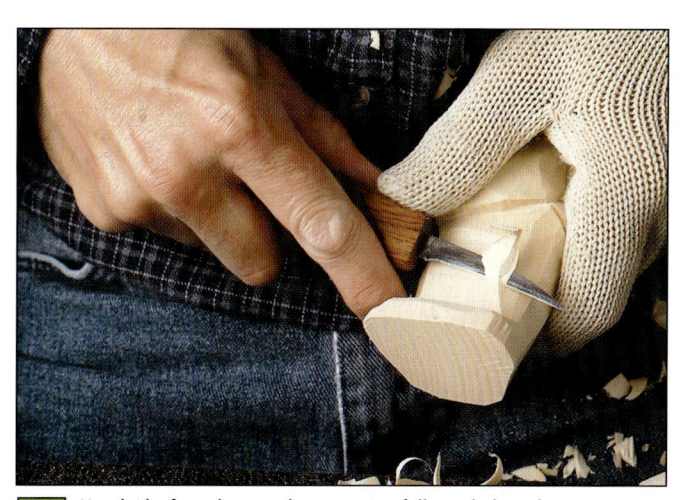

16 Use the knife to clean up the pants. Carefully work them down to a finished size.

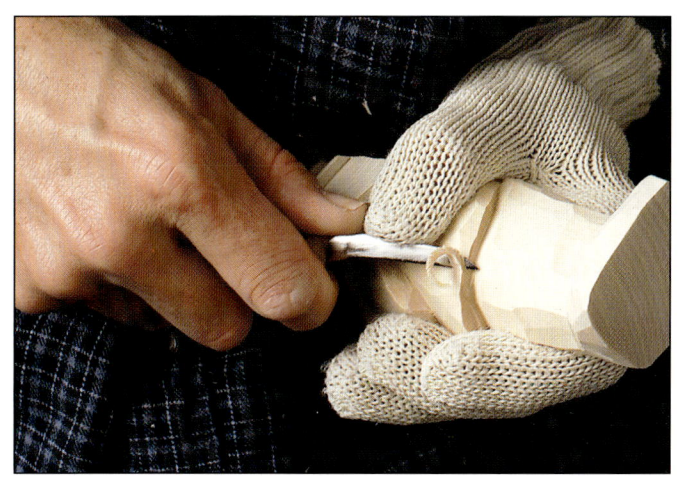

17 Use the knife to clean up and shape the coat hem. The hem should be rounded to follow the flow of the coat. The edges of the hem should be rounded as well. With the 8mm v-tool, cut a line around and above the hem to separate it from the coat.

18 Still using an 8mm v-tool, cut a line around the bottom of the pants to separate the hem from the boots. Use the knife to clean up and shape the boots.

Carving Snowmen and Santas — Chapter Three

SANTA STEP-BY-STEP

19 Go back to the head. Clean up and shape the tassel. Shape the head and hat area to a finished size.

20 After the head is proportioned to a finished size, pencil in the legs, front and back. Be careful to center the lines with the center of the body.

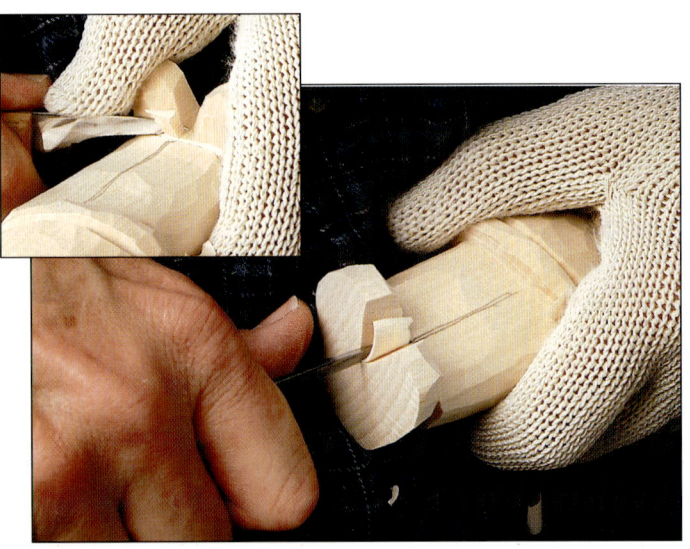

21 With the knife, separate the boots until the toes of the boots are approximately 3/8 in. apart. Shape and finish the boots.

22 With a 6mm v-tool cut the leg lines down to the boots. Just cut simple deep lines to distinguish the legs.

23 Now cut a center line on the bottom of the piece to separate the shoes. Next, cut across both shoe soles to form the heels. Deepen the heel cuts and do some clean up with the v-tool.

24 After the pants are shaped to size, use a 4mm v-tool to cut the cuffs around bottom of the pants. Simply cut a line with the v-tool to form the cuff.

Chapter Three

Carving Snowmen and Santas

SANTA STEP-BY-STEP

25 With the same v-tool, cut around the shoes to form the soles of the shoes.

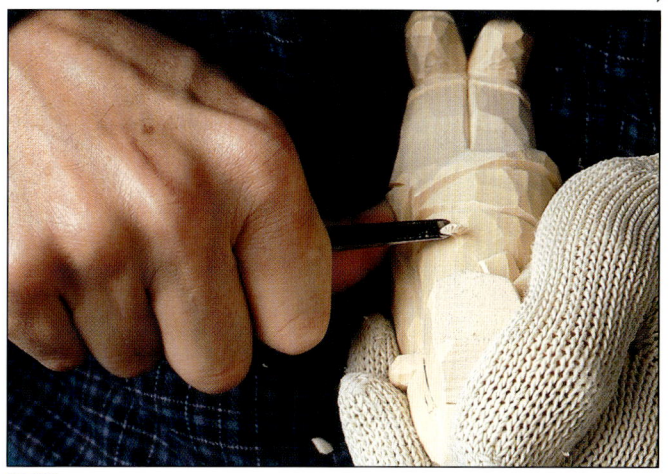

26 With a 4mm v-tool, cut two lines across the coat to make a wide belt.

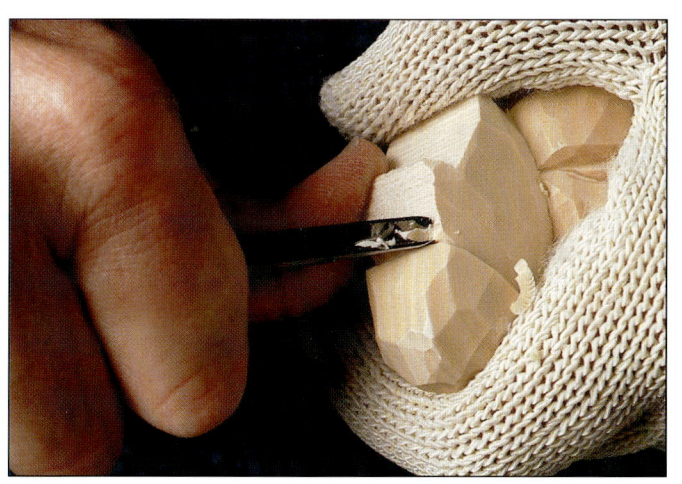

27 "Snug" the v-tool up against the hat and make a clean cut all the way across. This cut will separate the hat cuff from the top of the eyebrows.

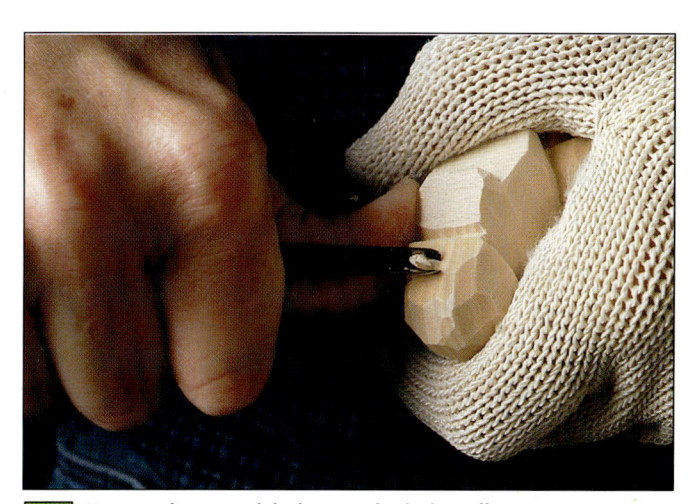

28 Now cut a line around the hat to make the hat cuff.

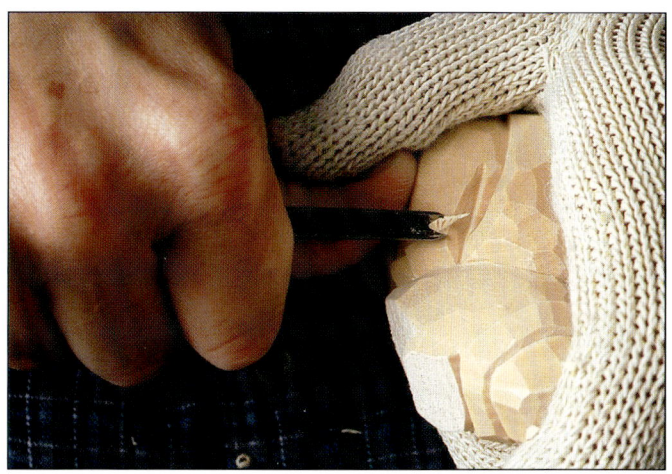

29 Make a cut across the coat sleeve close to the bottom of the sleeve. This cut will form the cuff. There will be a mitten showing between the cuff and the beard.

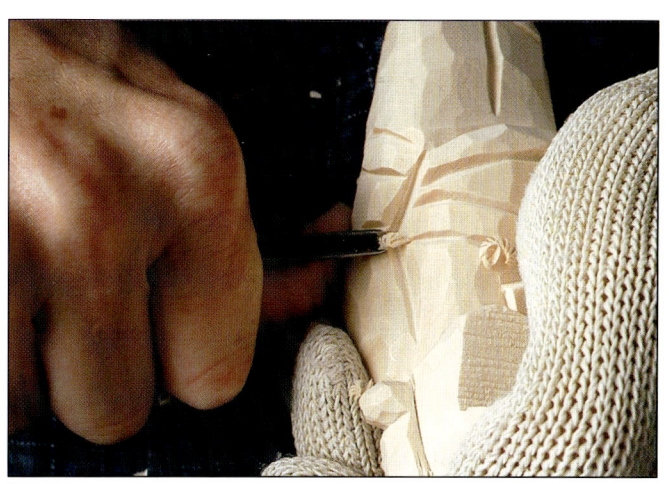

30 Notice the cut that forms the cuff. Where the hand enters the pocket, make another simple cut similar to that cut. None of the hand will be showing; the cuff will join the pocket. Make a couple of cuts at the bend of the arm to create wrinkles in the sleeve.

Carving Snowmen and Santas — **Chapter Three**

SANTA STEP-BY-STEP

31 Still using the 4mm v-tool, make horizontal cuts at the crotch on the front and back of the piece. You can cut more wrinkles anywhere they look natural. Wrinkles are nothing more than simple cuts, but they really add to your carving.

32 With the knife, remove some wood above and below the belt to raise the belt above the coat.

33 Now with the dimensions of the piece almost finished, let's begin work on the face. Mark a center line to center the nose on the face. Pencil in a triangle-shaped nose that is wider at the bottom of the nose and more narrow at the top. With a knife, cut straight into these lines.

34 With the knife, trim wood away from each side of the nose. Remove enough wood to make the cheeks level with the rest of the face. I'm using a knife that has been worn down to the size of a detail knife.

35 Trim the bottom corner on both sides of the nose. This will form the nostril areas on each side.

36 Now we can shape and clean up the nose and the cheeks. Keep checking the dimensions of the nose so the nose will match the size of the face. Trim it as necessary.

Chapter Three | Carving Snowmen and Santas

SANTA STEP-BY-STEP

37 Pencil on the mustache lines. Put a little "action" into the mustache by dropping the line down and then curving it up at the ends. Notice that I penciled on a centerline under the nose. This line helps to keep the facial features centered.

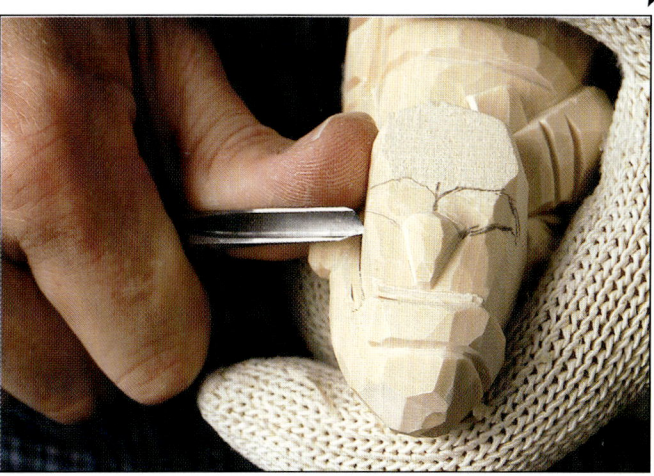

38 With the 4mm v-tool, cut the mustache lines. Do a little trimming with the v-tool to get the mustache sized just right.

39 Now deepen these cuts to raise the mustache. The mustache should be raised fairly high off the face.

40 Use the 4mm v-tool to make a simple mouth or lower lip by cutting across and under the mouth. Make the cut in a half-moon shape. Do a little trimming, and the mouth is done.

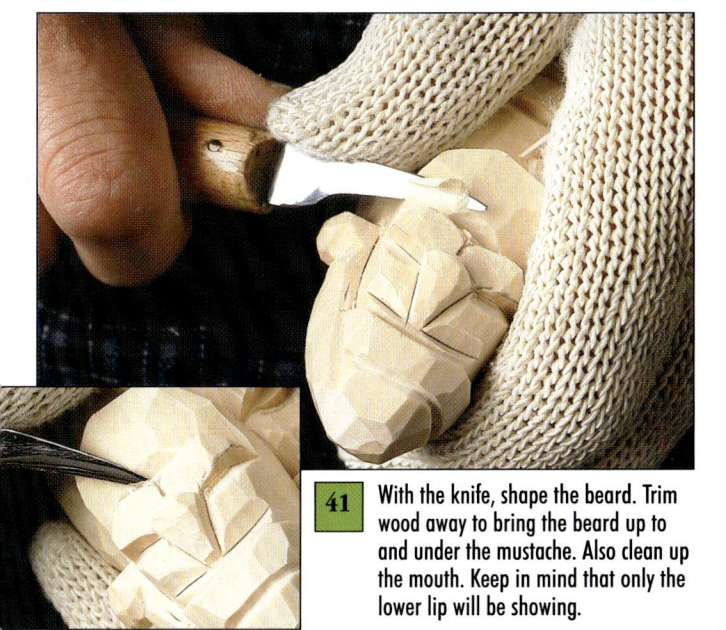

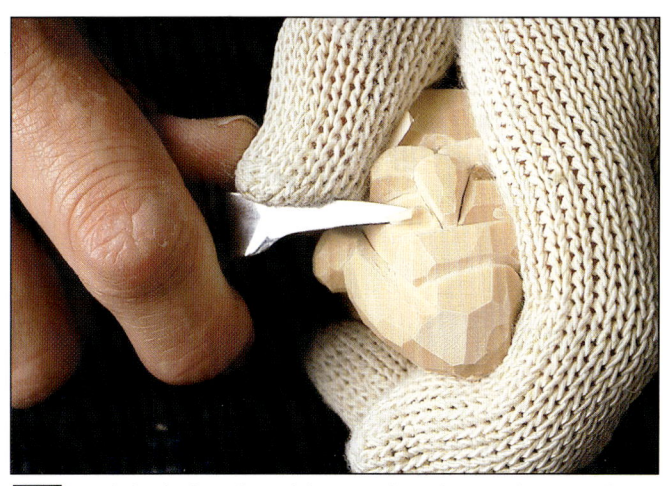

41 With the knife, shape the beard. Trim wood away to bring the beard up to and under the mustache. Also clean up the mouth. Keep in mind that only the lower lip will be showing.

42 Finish the cheeks and round them just above the mustache. Notice the straight knife cuts on each side of the nose. These help to separate the nose from the cheeks and give a cleaner-looking face.

Carving Snowmen and Santas — 23 — Chapter Three

SANTA STEP-BY-STEP

43 Clean up the mustache to give it a nice, rounded look. You can see here how those cuts on each side of the nose give a good clean separation of the nose and cheeks.

44 Now finish shaping and sizing the beard. Make some deeper cuts, as shown here, to give the beard a wavy look.

45 Use the knife tip to cut the hair line on each side of the face. Trim the face at this line to raise the hair line higher than the face.

46 With the 3mm veining gouge, scoop out the eye sockets on both sides. Just scoop out nice shallow sockets. Be careful to make them the same size.

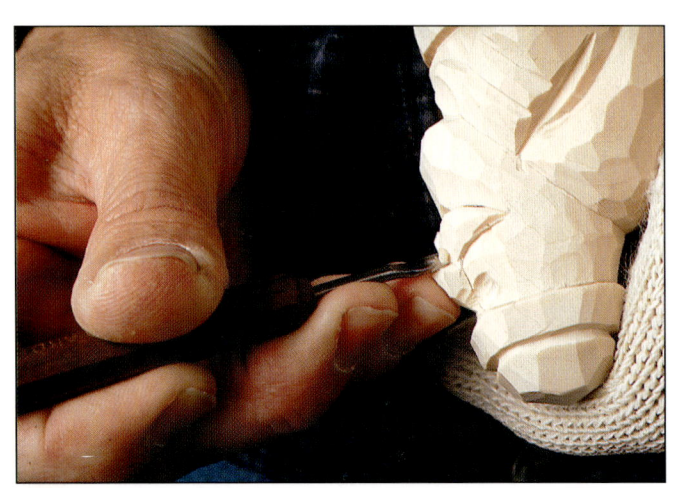

47 With the same veining gouge, scoop out the nostrils on each side of the nose. Also scoop out a small area on the top of the nose above the nostrils. Looking at your own nose in the mirror will help you with this step.

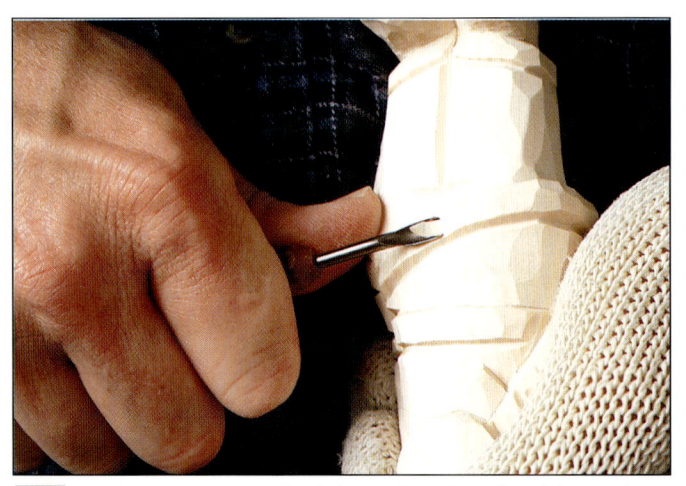

48 Use the veining gouge to finish the coat hem, the cuffs and the tassel. Remove small scoops of wood close together to give the appearance of fur.

Chapter Three — Carving Snowmen and Santas

SANTA STEP-BY-STEP

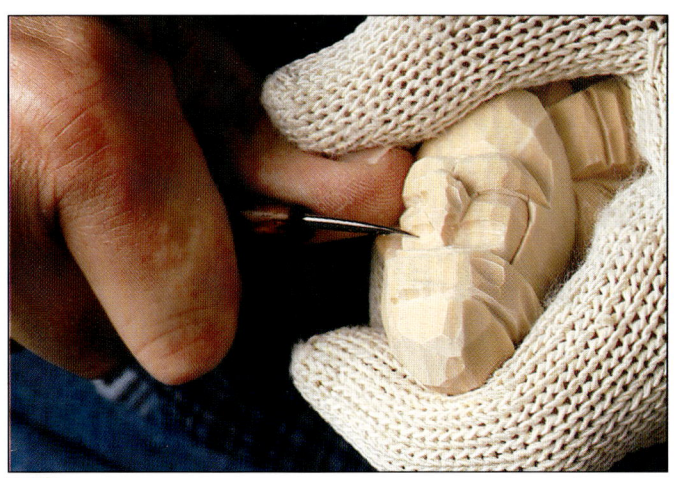

49 Now you're ready to carve the eyes. Most carvers would agree that the eyes are the most difficult part of a carving. This method is about the simplest I've found. Here I didn't pencil in the eyes, but you may want to do that before you begin cutting. Make straight cuts horizontally in the eye socket with a fine detail knife. Take care to keep them even. These cuts will become the top of the lower eyelid.

50 With the horizontal cuts in place, make a half-moon cut above the horizontal lines. Pencil in the lines to ensure the sizes are correct. It's easy to make the eyes too big. These half-moon cuts are the eyeball. Plant your thumb to provide control of the blade. Gently push the blade tip into the wood—deep enough only to cut the surface of the wood—then slowly cut the half-moon on top of the horizontal line.

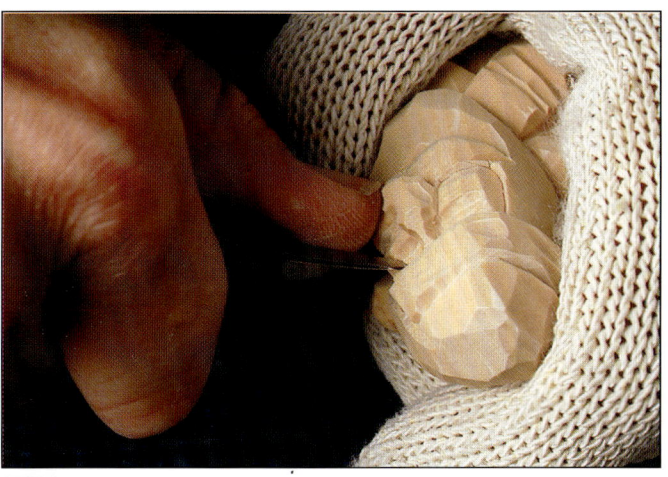

51 After the half-moon cuts are made, trim the outside edges of the half-moon eyeball. Don't trim too much wood—just enough to round the eyeball.

52 Compare the dimensions of the eyeballs until they match and appear to have a relaxed look.

53 To finish the eyes, use a 2mm v-tool to make a horizontal cut under the lower eyelid. This cut will have a slight half-moon shape curving upward to each corner of the eye. Be careful though. Just a slight curve is all you need. This cut will form the lower eyelid.

54 With the same 2mm v-tool, cut the mustache hairs. Notice how the cuts flow downward and outward. Also make one simple cut on the forehead to separate the eyebrows.

Carving Snowmen and Santas — 25 — Chapter Three

SANTA STEP-BY-STEP

55 Now cut the whisker lines in the beard and lines to show strands of hair. Stagger the cuts with different lengths and depths to give the appearance of flowing hair.

56 With a 4mm v-tool, cut some wrinkle lines in the end of the sack.

57 Use a fine-tip detail knife to cut the belt buckle. Simply cut a square inside the buckle and trim the inside edges of the square. Look Santa over one last time for any last minute adjustments that you might have overlooked.

58 Now for the finishing touch. With the 2mm v-tool, sign the bottom of your finished piece.

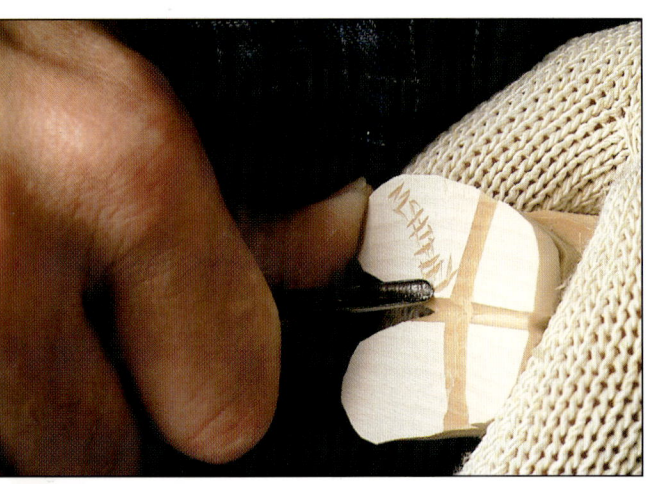

59 All the carving is complete.

Chapter Three — Carving Snowmen and Santas

PAINTING

SANTA STEP-BY-STEP

1 Before painting the piece, lightly sand it with 220-grit sandpaper to remove any surface dirt and to give the piece a worn look.

2 Paint the eyeballs white with the 4/0 spotter brush. I always paint the eyeballs first so the flesh paint will not bleed into the eye.

3 With the spotter brush paint the eyebrows white.

4 Paint the face with a flesh color. Use a #4 blender brush on the larger areas. You might want to use the spotter on the lips and around the eyes.

5 For the sack, use thicket green with a #8 shader. Use a #4 shader for the smaller areas of the sack, around the hair line and around the mitten.

6 Use licorice black on the belt with a #2 shader. Use the spotter brush to reach the inside surfaces of the belt buckle. Also paint the boots black with a #6 shader.

Carving Snowmen and Santas   Chapter Three

SANTA STEP-BY-STEP

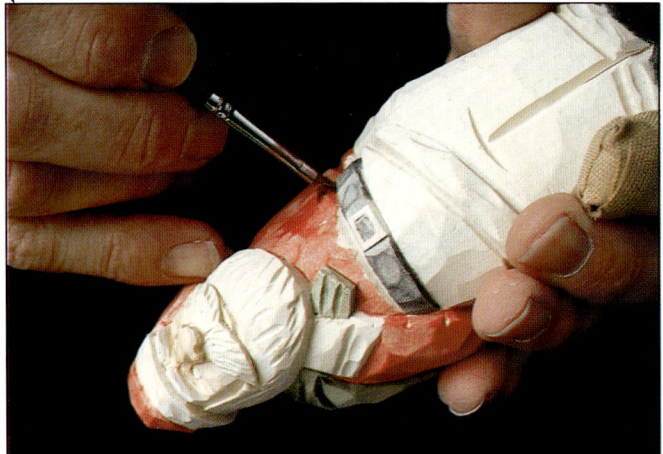

7 There are a lot of red colors, but I like cadmium red medium for a good "Santa red." Use a #2 shader on the smaller areas, and the #4 shader on the larger areas. Red is a harsh color, so don't just paint it on. I use circular blending strokes to make sure the paint covers evenly.

8 With the #2 shader, paint the mitten on the right hand with hunter green.

9 Paint all of the cuffs and the coat hem white. Use the #4 shader on the large areas. The #2 shader works best on smaller areas, such as the tassel and the hat cuff.

10 Use the same white color on the beard, mustache and hair. These areas are critical, so use a #2 shader. Be careful at this point, if any of the colors haven't dried. It's very easy to touch a wet color and smear it into another color.

11 Now we're ready for the part most carvers dread: painting the eyes. Notice here how I plant my fingers to control the brush. Use coffee bean brown straight from the bottle and a spotter brush to make a small dot on the eye. Carefully enlarge the dot. Take your time and check the size of the eye often. Don't get the eye too large. Now dot the other eye and adjust them both until they are even and have a relaxed look. Don't cover all of the white eyeball; you are only painting the iris on the eyeball.

12 Let the brown on the eyes dry for about 30 minutes. Use white straight from the bottle and a sharp toothpick to highlight the eyes. Just dip the toothpick in the white paint and touch it to the top of the brown iris. A small dot is all it takes. Notice how this highlight brings the eyes to life.

Chapter Three

Carving Snowmen and Santas

SANTA STEP-BY-STEP

13 Let the piece dry for at least one hour. Notice how the colors have a harsh, dry appearance? I always use a stain, which will penetrate the wood to make the carving water resistant and soften the appearance of the paint.

14 Now simply dip one half of the piece and let the excess drip back into the jar.

15 Dip the other half and let the piece drip for a short time. Check the recessed areas, such as the eyes, for good coverage. Now towel the piece dry with paper towels. The stain is difficult to towel dry. The piece will still have a slight oily feel, but it will dry in approximately 24 hours. The odor will disappear shortly.

16 That's about all we can do for Santa. The rest is up to him now. When he's finished with his deliveries, he'll be back on your shelf for you to enjoy until duty calls again.

Carving Snowmen and Santas — 29 — Chapter Three

SNOWMAN IN A TOP HAT

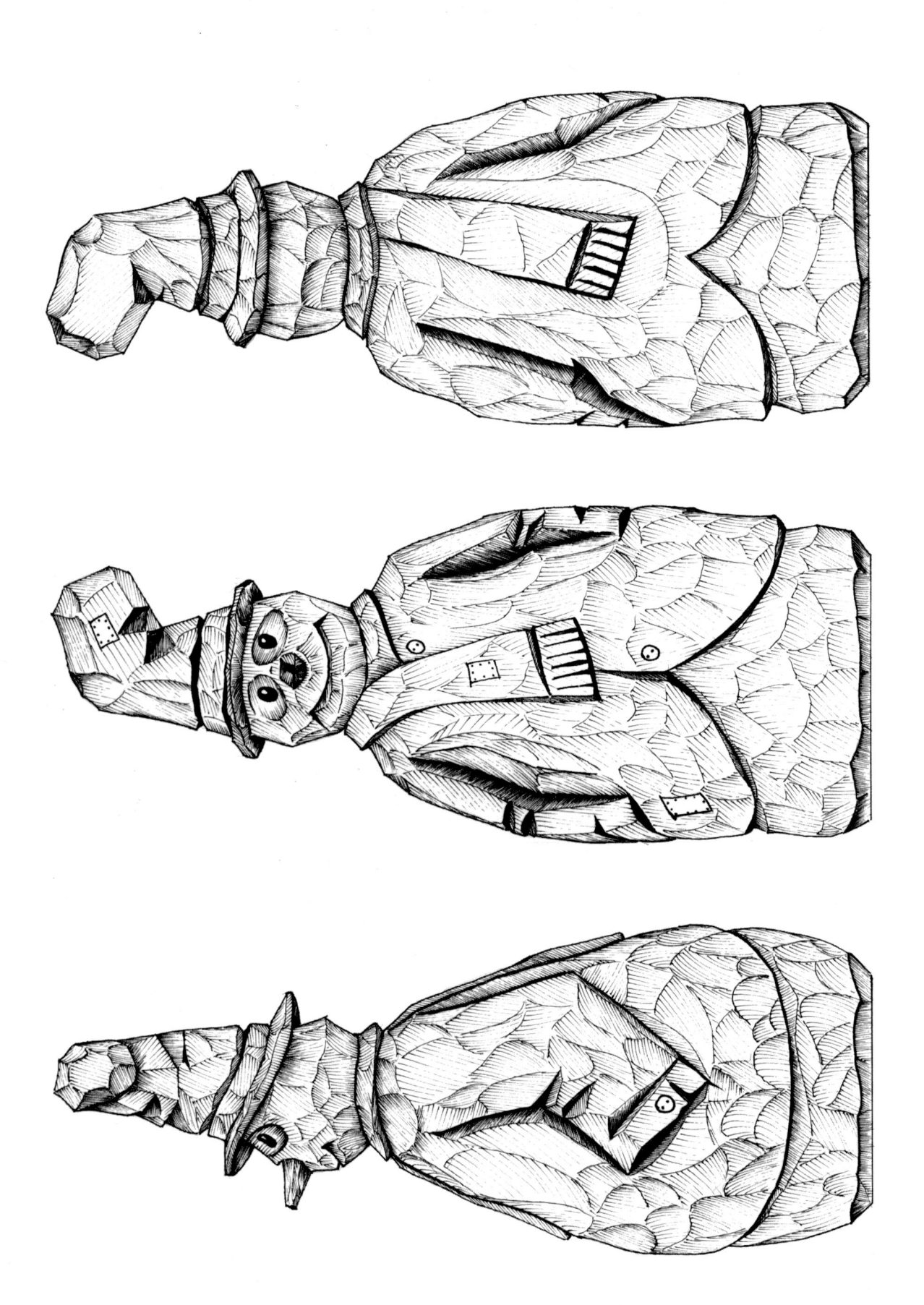

© Mike Shipley

Patterns

Carving Snowmen and Santas

SNOWMAN IN A TOP HAT

Carving snowmen is my favorite subject, probably because of the endless possibilities. A snowman can wear practically any type of clothing, or no clothing at all. This pattern also works well in a smaller size. (Height: 6 1/8")

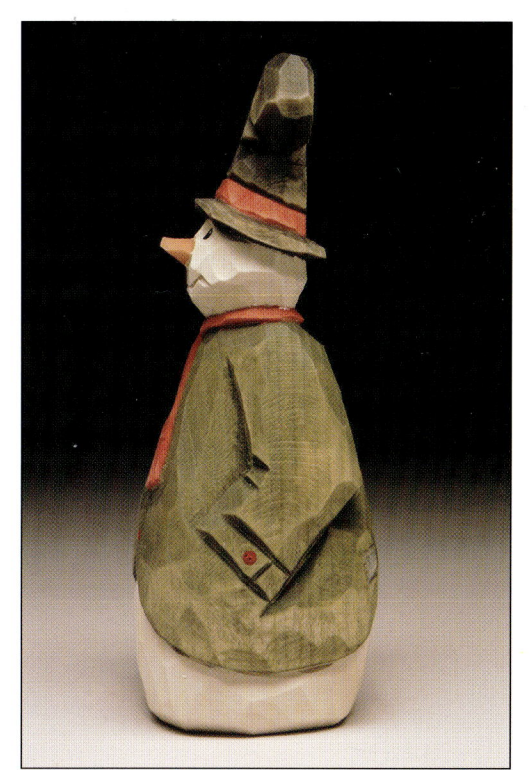

Carving Snowmen and Santas — *Patterns*

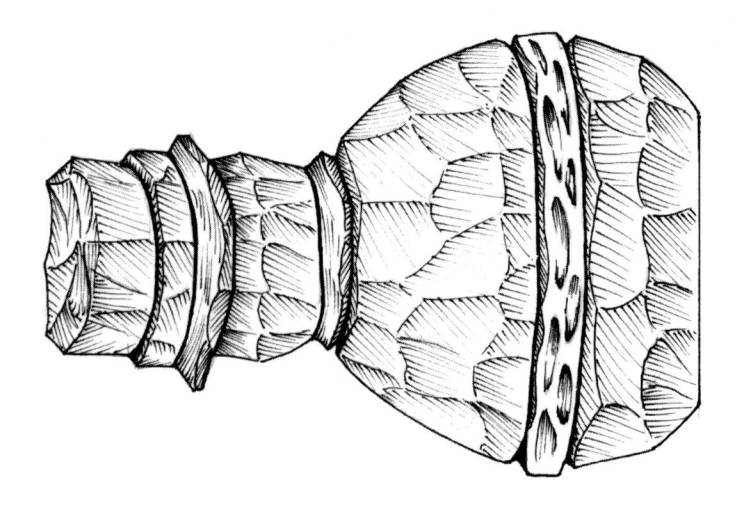

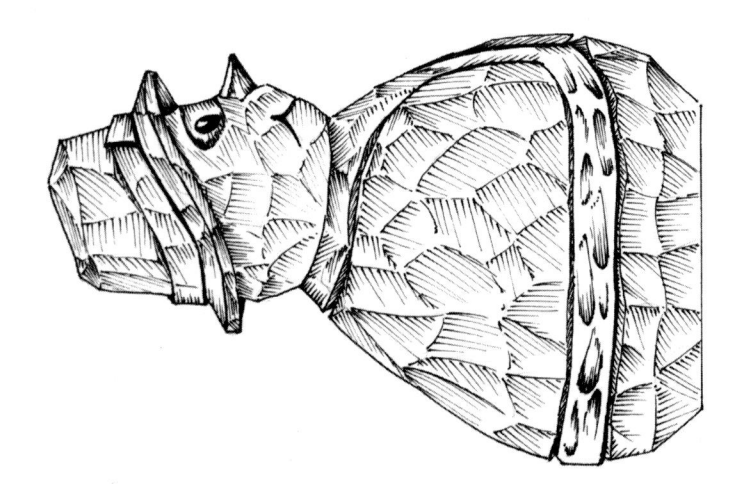

SNOWLADY

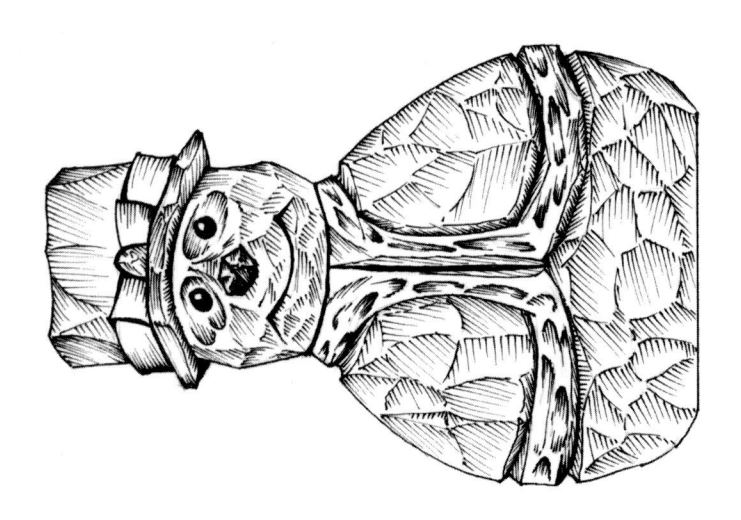

© Mike Shipley

SNOWLADY

This little snowlady likes to keep company with the snowman in the step-by-step section. She should, because after all, they are the same pattern. This snowlady proves just how versatile snowmen can be. (Height: 3 1/2")

Carving Snowmen and Santas   33   Patterns

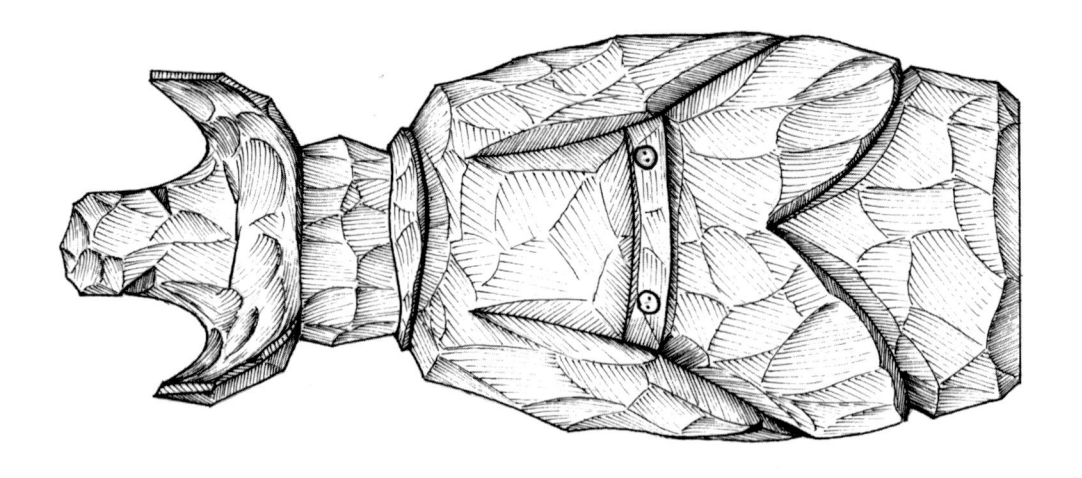

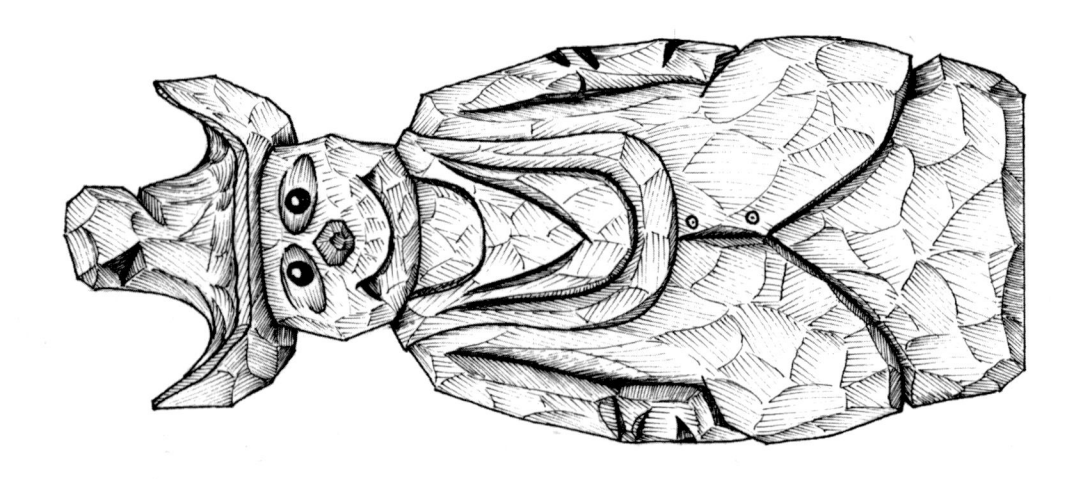

COWBOY SNOWMAN

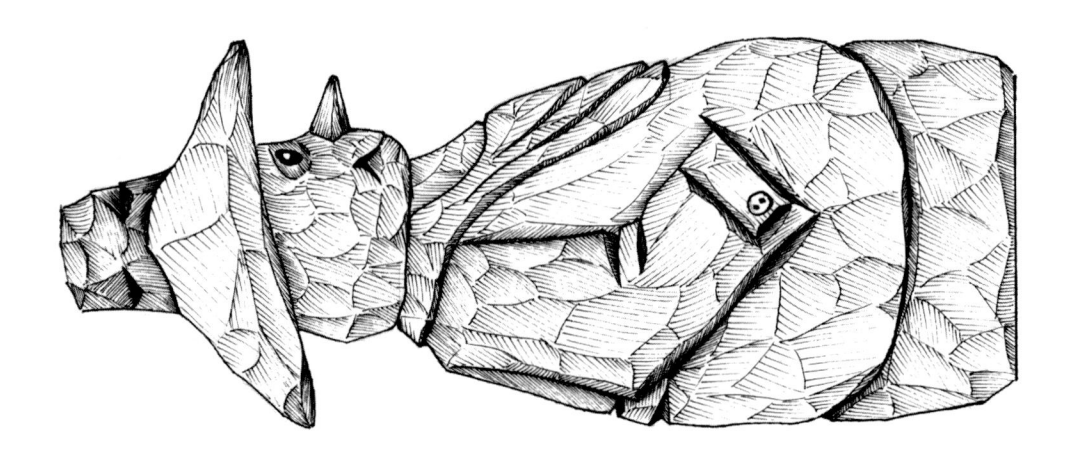

© Mike Shipley

Patterns

Carving Snowmen and Santas

COWBOY SNOWMAN

I know that a snowman would melt out on the hot dusty trail, but this guy is fun to carve anyway. He is a good pick-me-up no matter where you live or what trail you follow. (Height: 5 1/4")

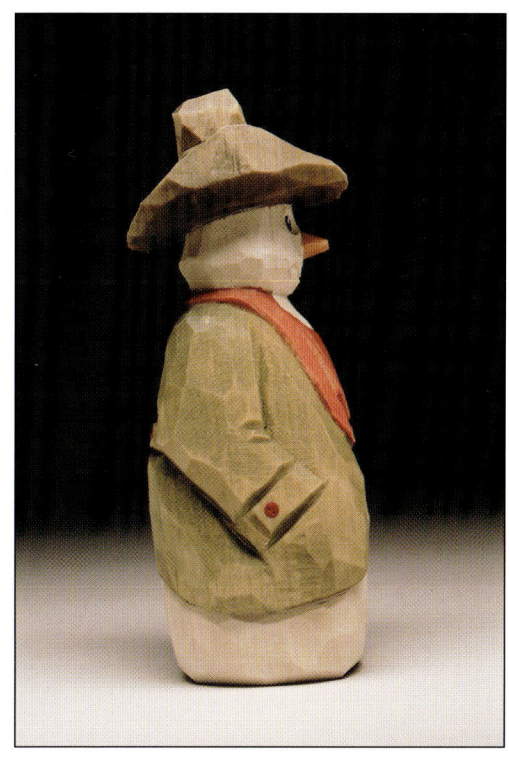

Carving Snowmen and Santas   Patterns

SNOWMAN & SANTA SPOONS

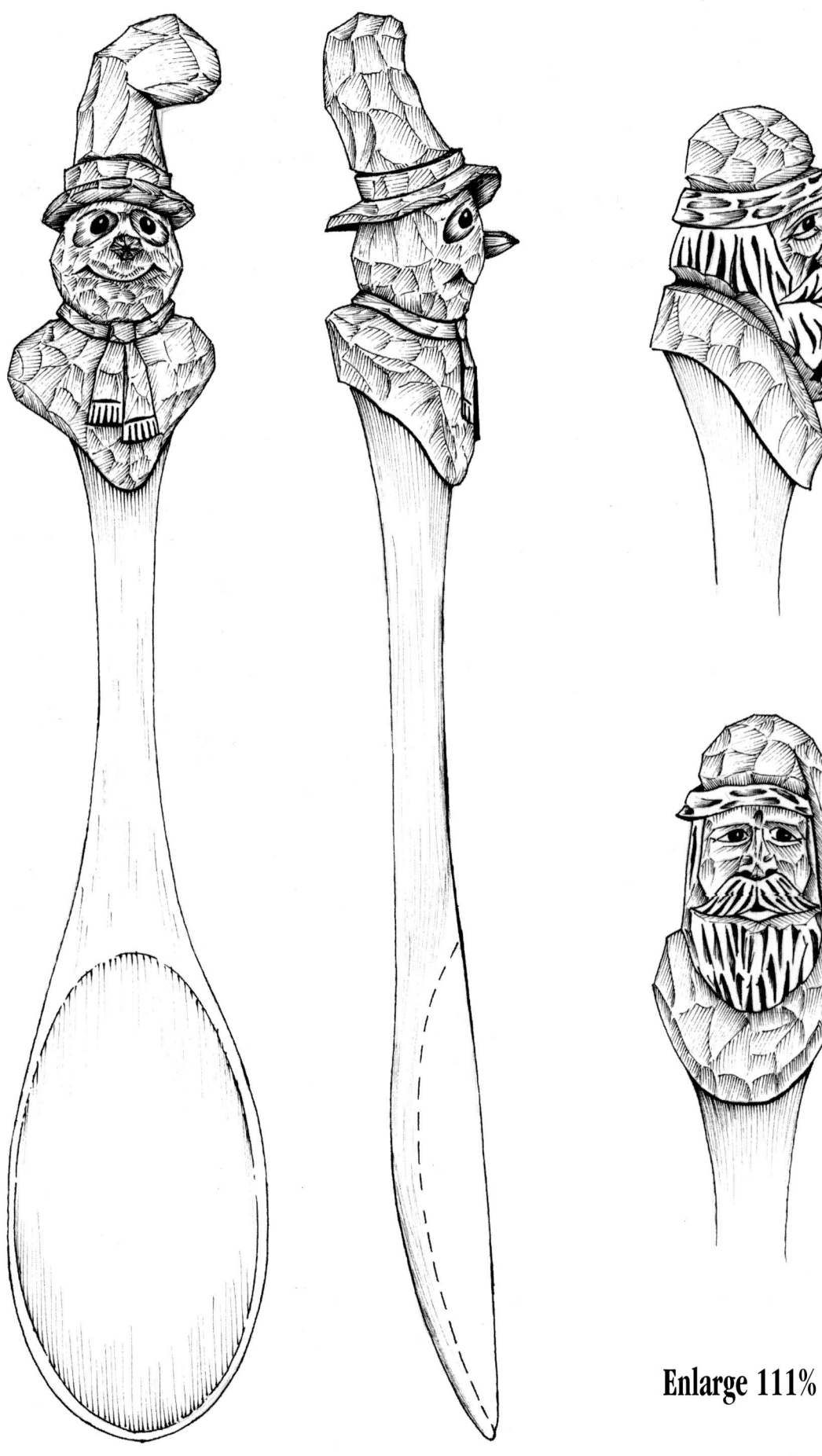

Enlarge 111%

© Mike Shipley

Patterns

Carving Snowmen and Santas

SNOWMAN & SANTA SPOONS

These spoons are not just for looks. Coat the spoons and handles with vegetable oil and start stirring your favorite soup or chili. Make sure to coat the spoons occasionally with oil and they will last a long time. (Height: 10 1/2")

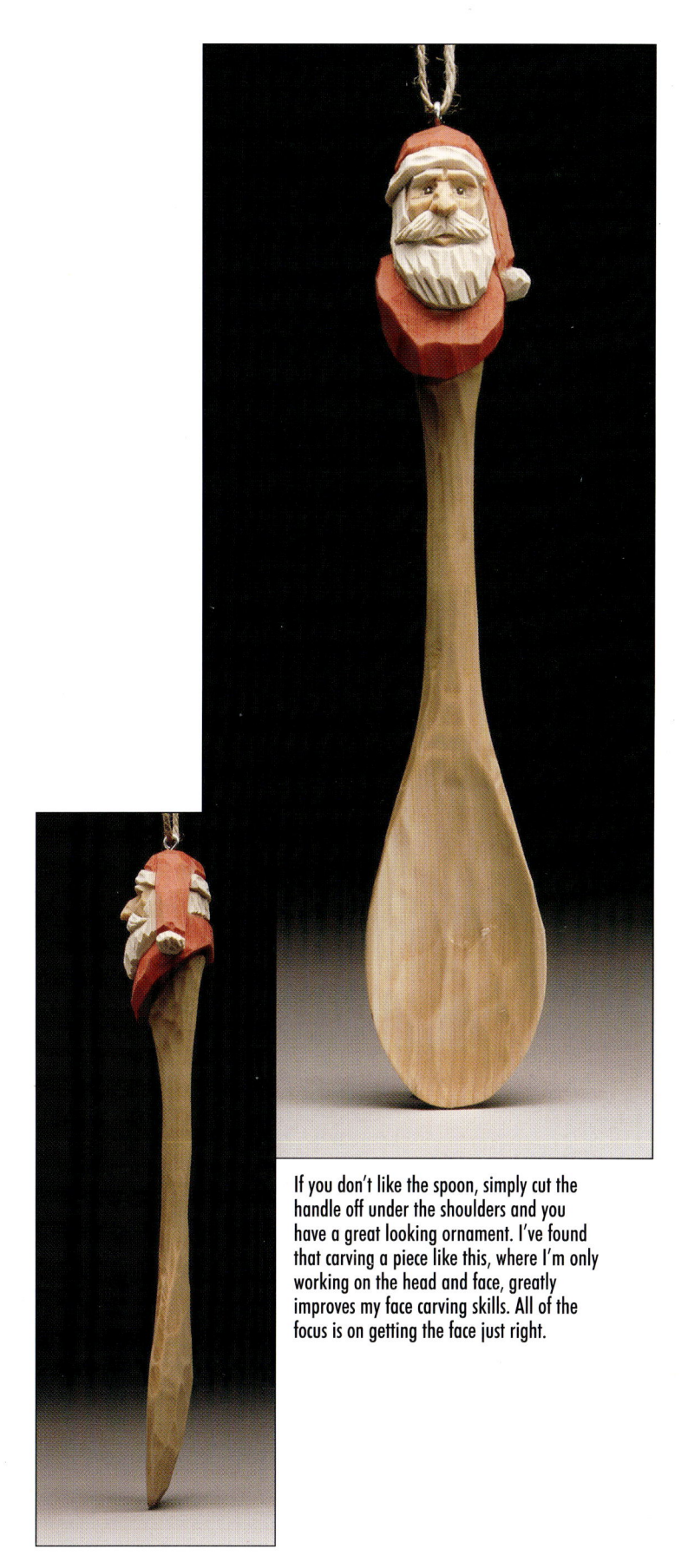

If you don't like the spoon, simply cut the handle off under the shoulders and you have a great looking ornament. I've found that carving a piece like this, where I'm only working on the head and face, greatly improves my face carving skills. All of the focus is on getting the face just right.

Carving Snowmen and Santas — Patterns

TRADITIONAL SANTA

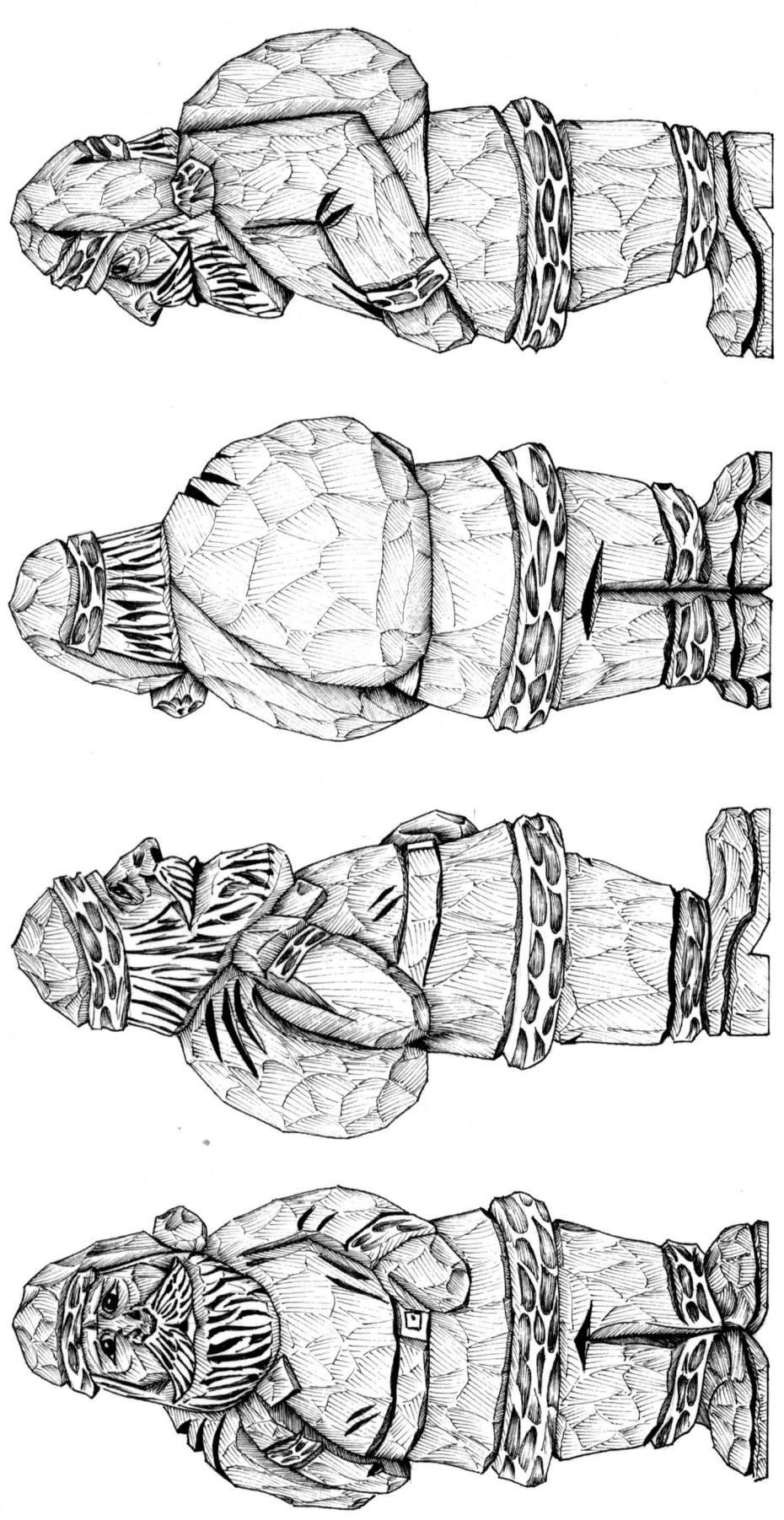

Enlarge 105%

© Mike Shipley

TRADITIONAL SANTA

This Santa is very similar to the project in Chapter 3. The mitten resting on the belt makes this piece a little more difficult. This Santa also looks very good in a smaller size. (Height: 5")

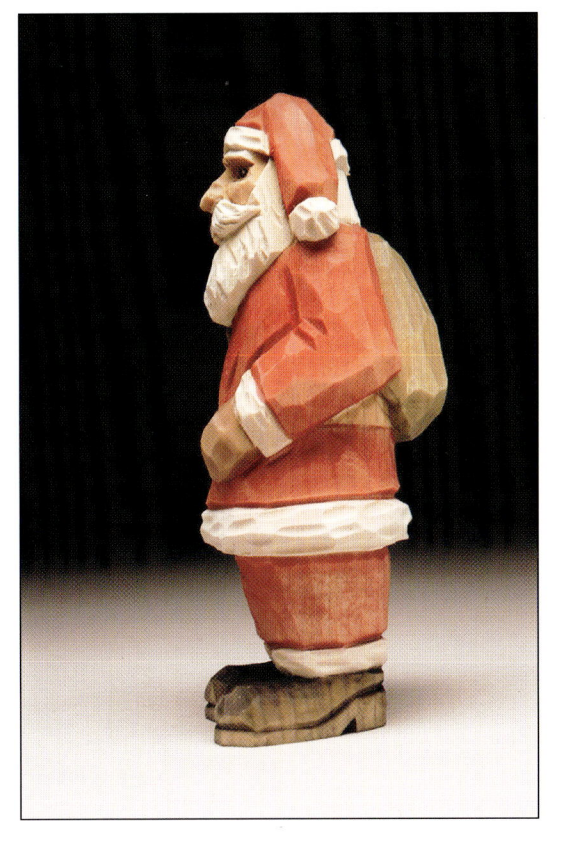

Carving Snowmen and Santas   Patterns

UNCLE SAM SANTA

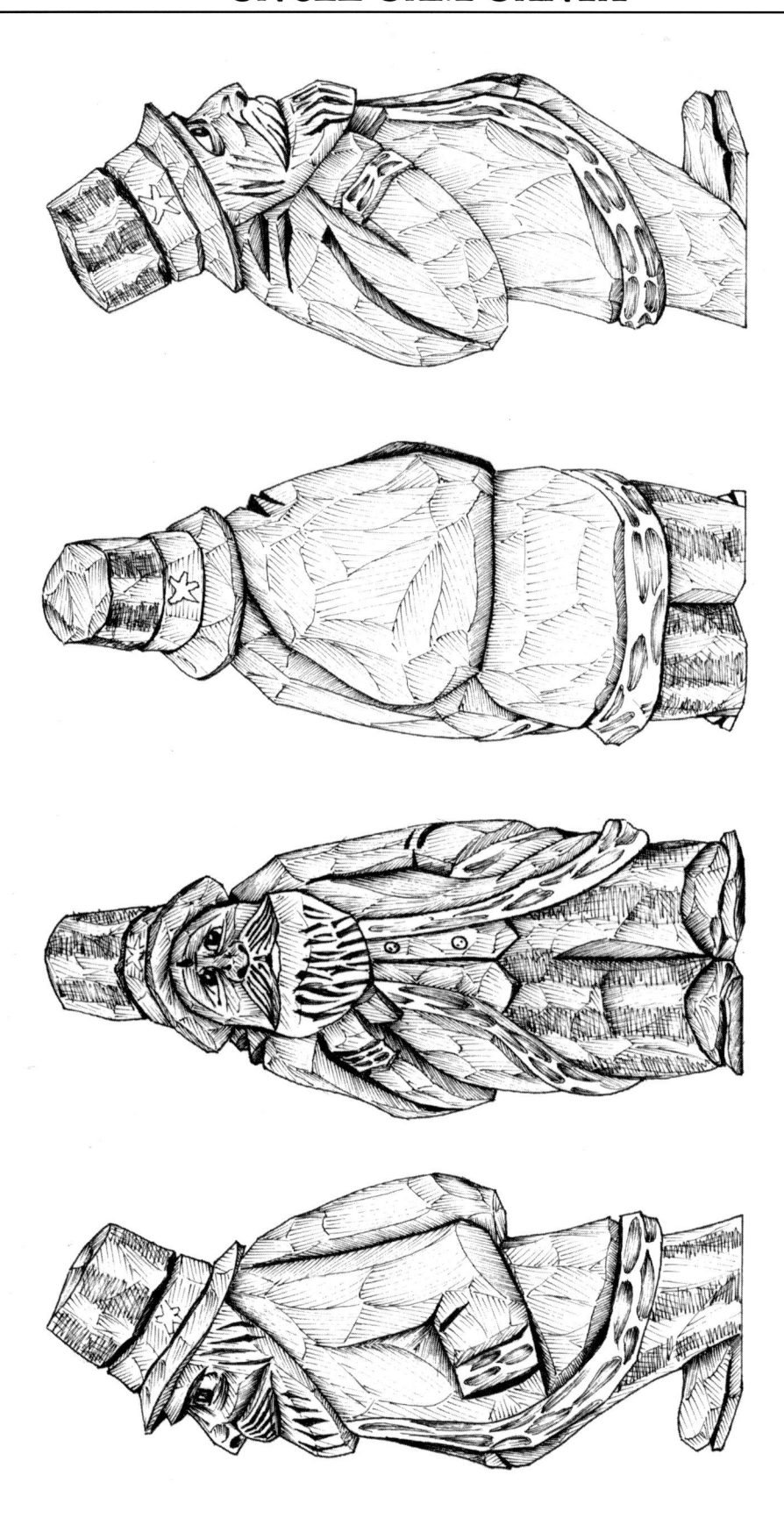

© Mike Shipley

Patterns

Carving Snowmen and Santas

UNCLE SAM SANTA

Here we have two Uncle Sams in one. Simply remove the sack, add a blue coat with tails, and you have an Uncle Sam for the Fourth of July. The stars are made with a sharp toothpick dipped in white paint. Simply dot the center of the star and then drag the paint out to form the five points of the star. (Height: 4 1/4")

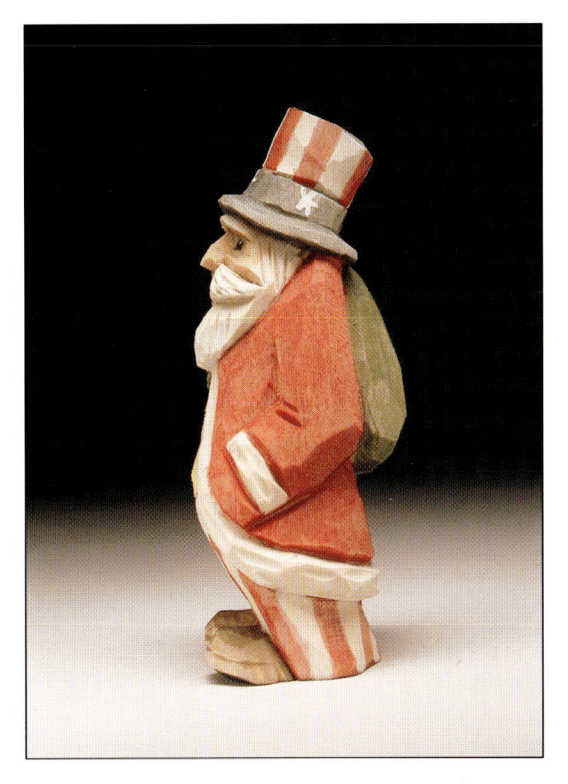

Carving Snowmen and Santas   Patterns

OLD WORLD SANTA

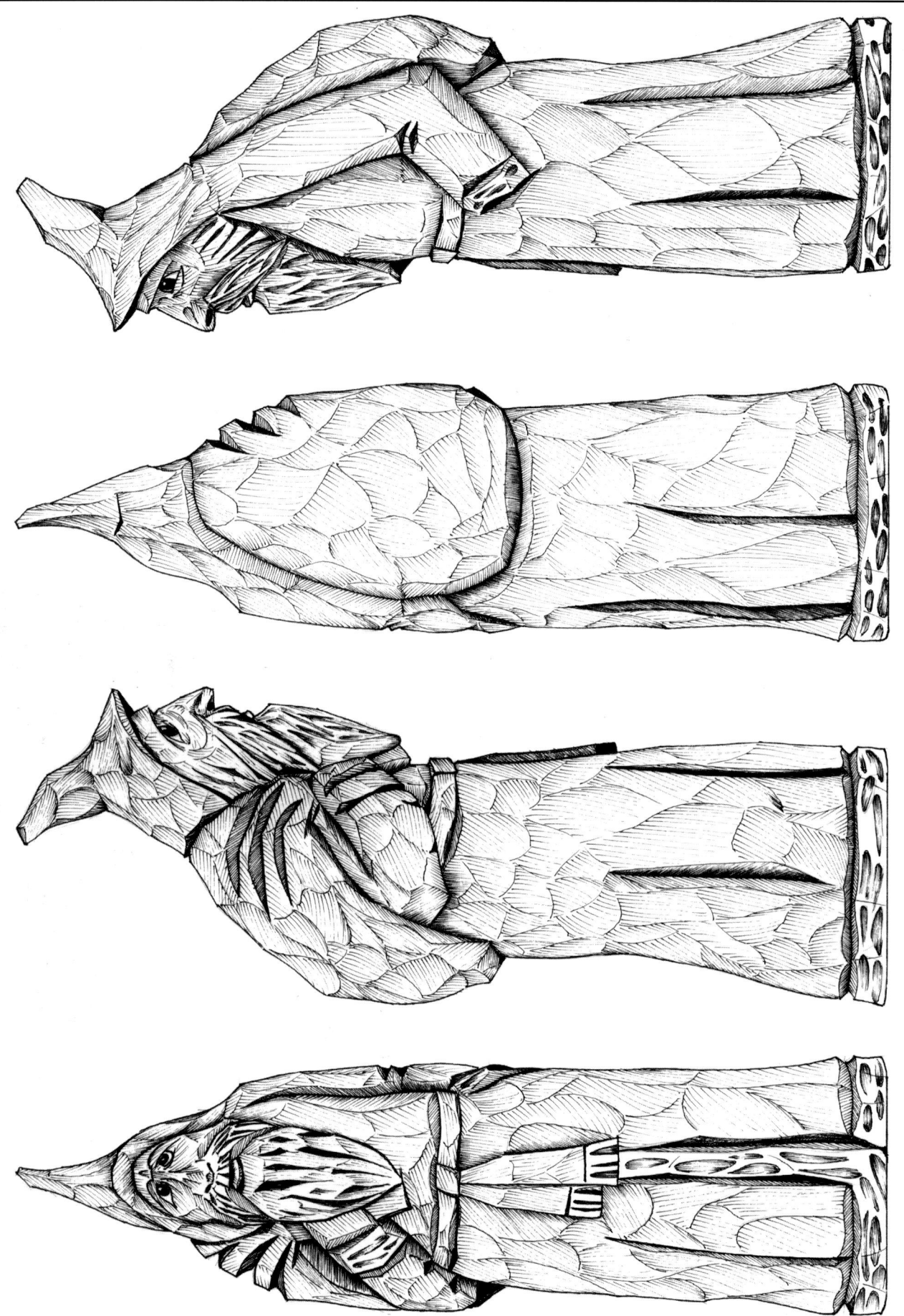

© Mike Shipley

Patterns — 42 — Carving Snowmen and Santas

OLD WORLD SANTA

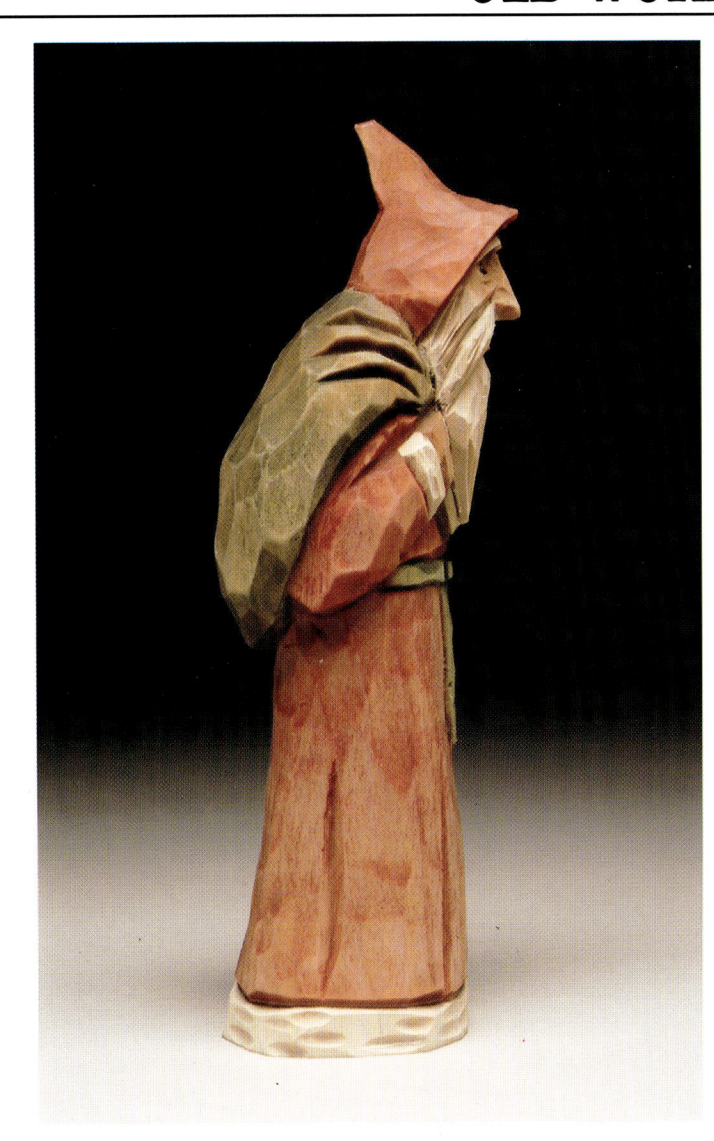

Notice how leaning forward adds character to this Santa. This also adds a little bit of difficulty because the grain direction changes from the body to the face. One hand in the pocket makes the carving flow more easily. (Height: 6 1/2")

Carving Snowmen and Santas　　43　　Patterns

SAINT NICHOLAS

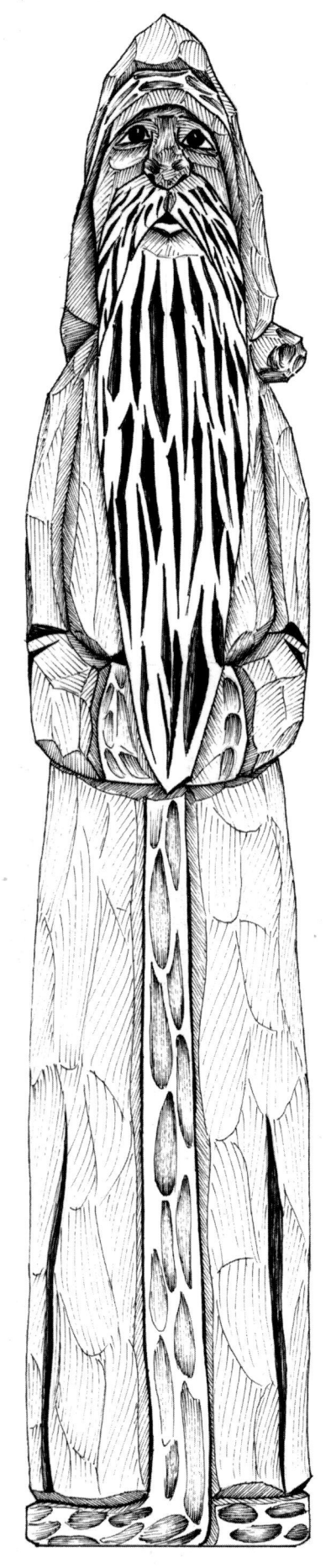

© Mike Shipley

Patterns

Carving Snowmen and Santas

SAINT NICHOLAS

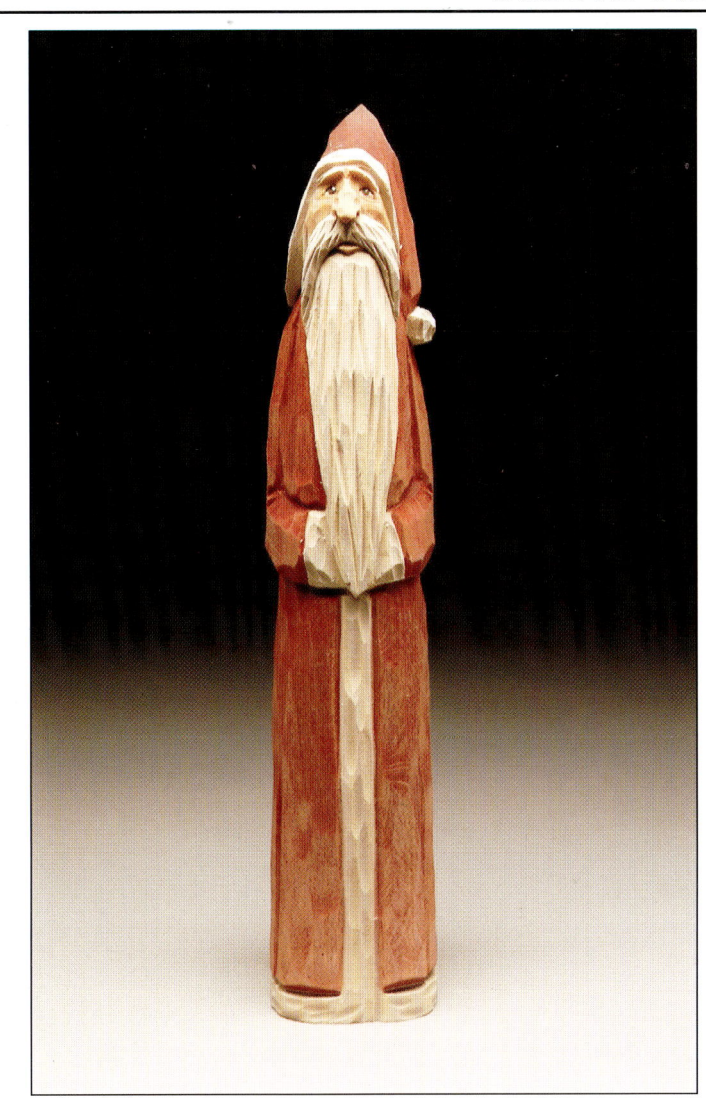

As you can see, this Santa is designed to be very easy to carve. The design of this pattern will enlarge very easily, in fact, the taller he is the better he'll look. A good size is 24". This Santa is intended to be tall and slim. (Height: 10 1/8")

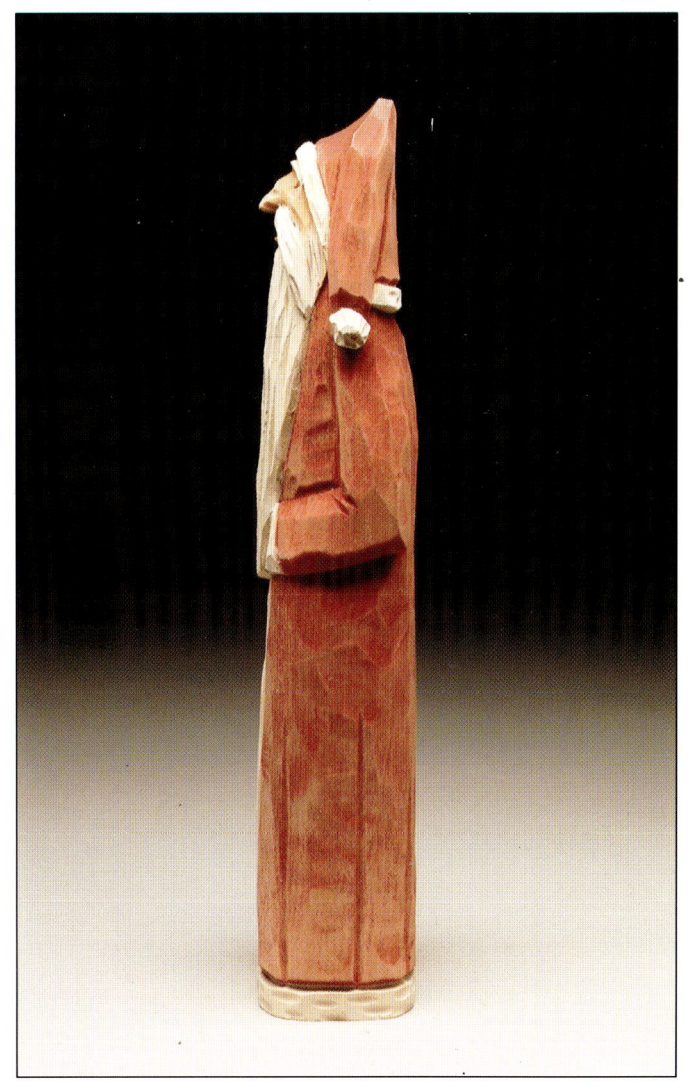

Carving Snowmen and Santas Patterns

WOODLAND SANTA

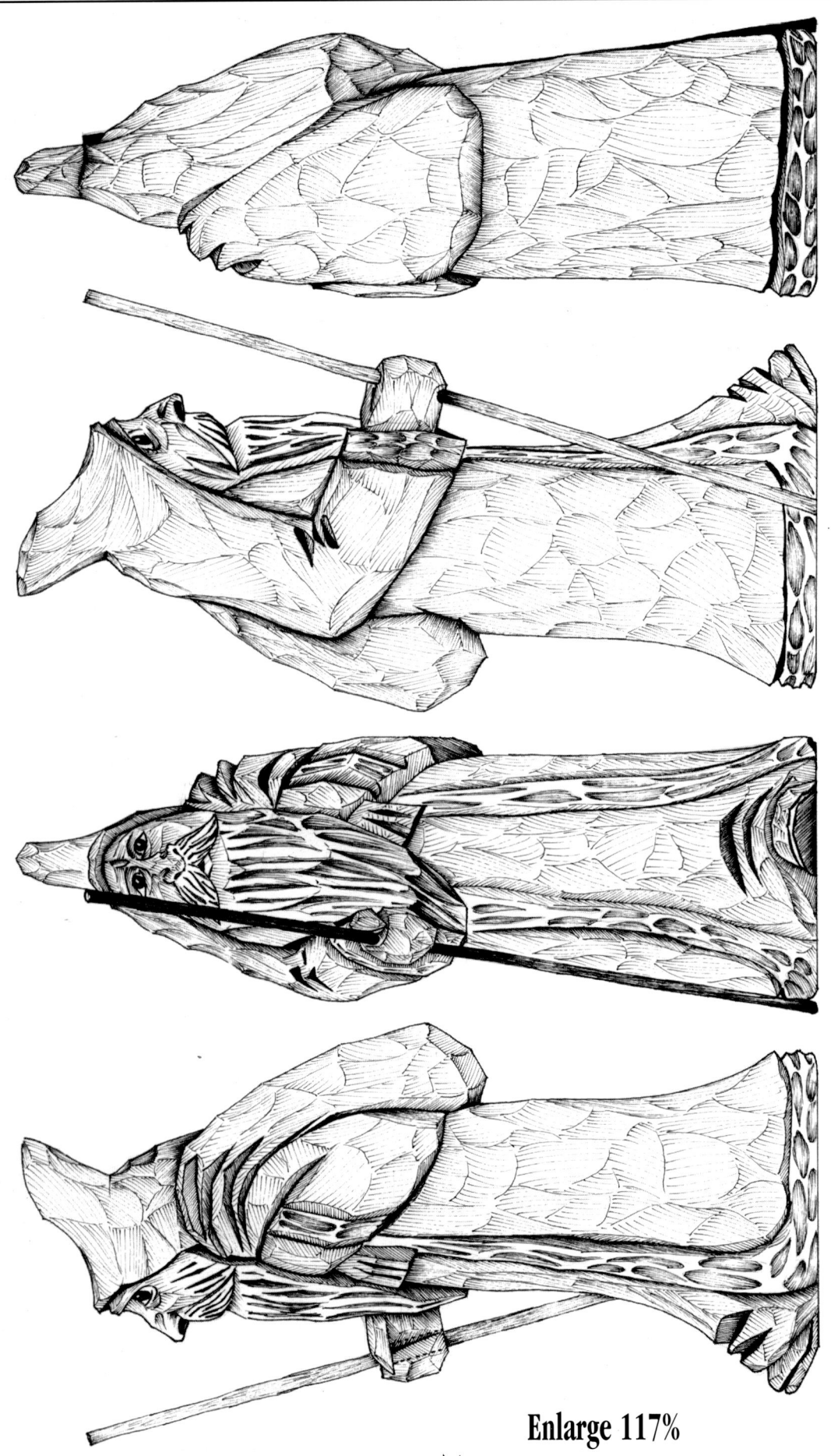

Enlarge 117%

© Mike Shipley

Carving Snowmen and Santas

WOODLAND SANTA

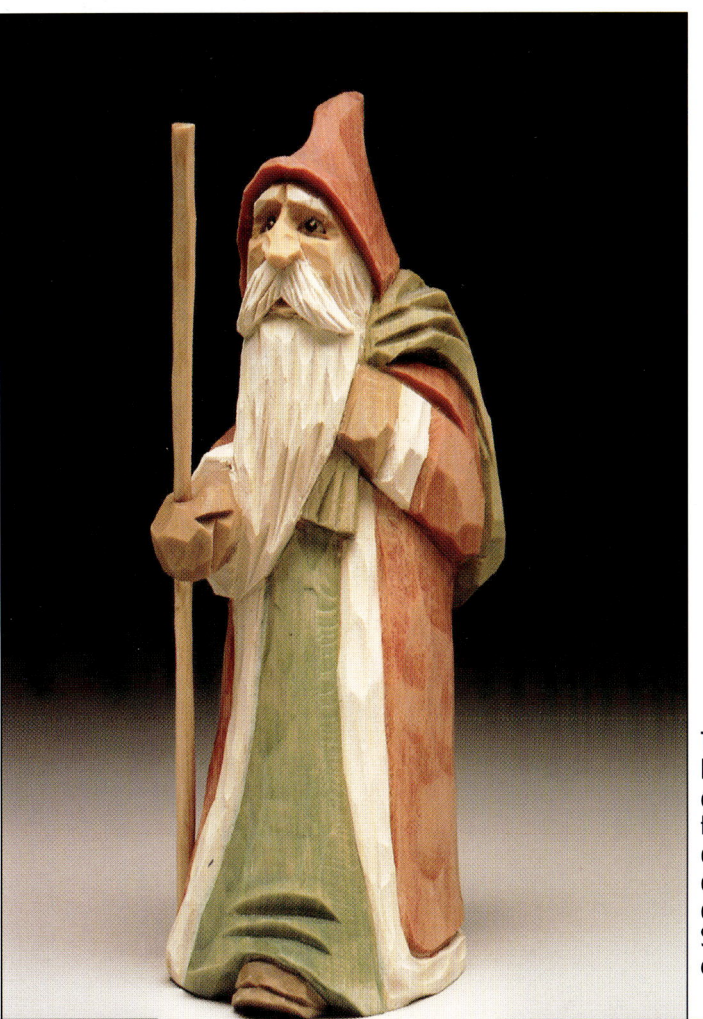

This Santa is not as difficult as he looks. The long flowing coat is very easy to carve. The shoe extending out from under the coat should give the appearance of walking. Carefully drill a small hole in the right-hand mitten and carve the staff to fit. I painted this Santa with a darker red than the red of a traditional Santa. (Height: 6 1/2")

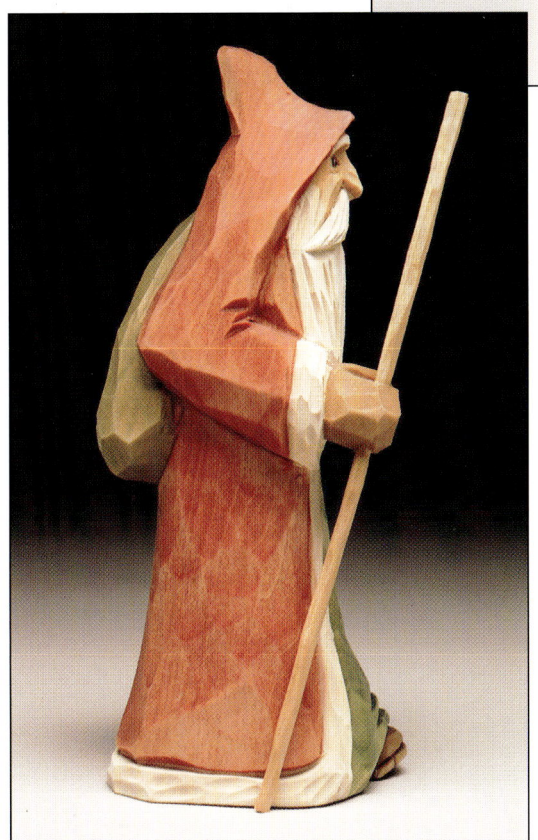

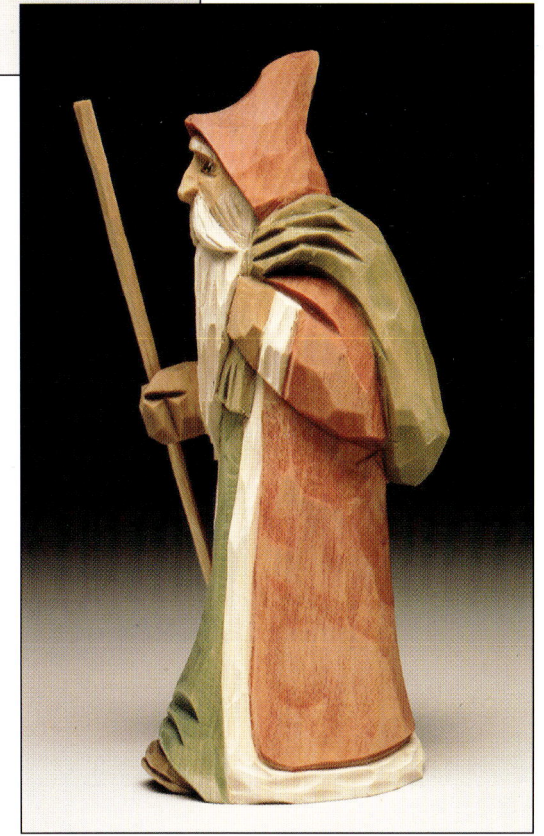

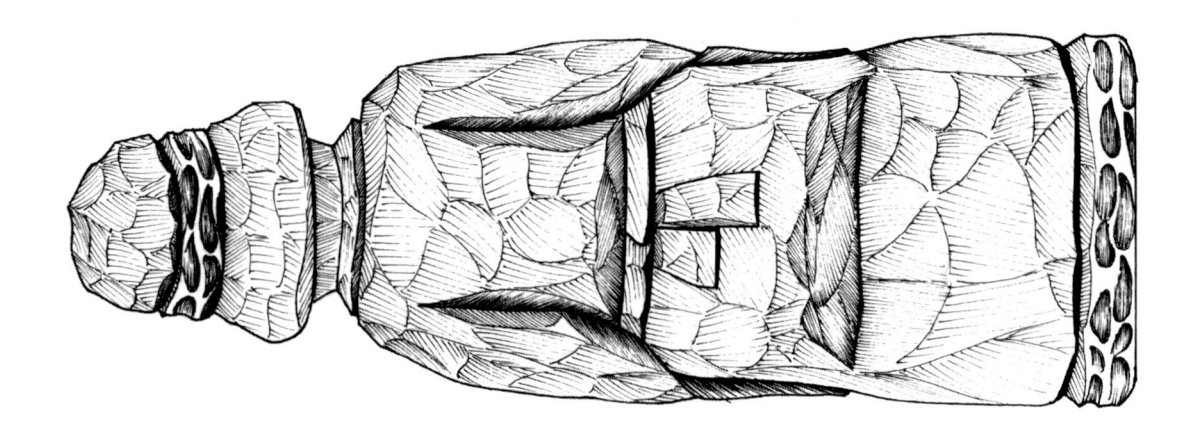

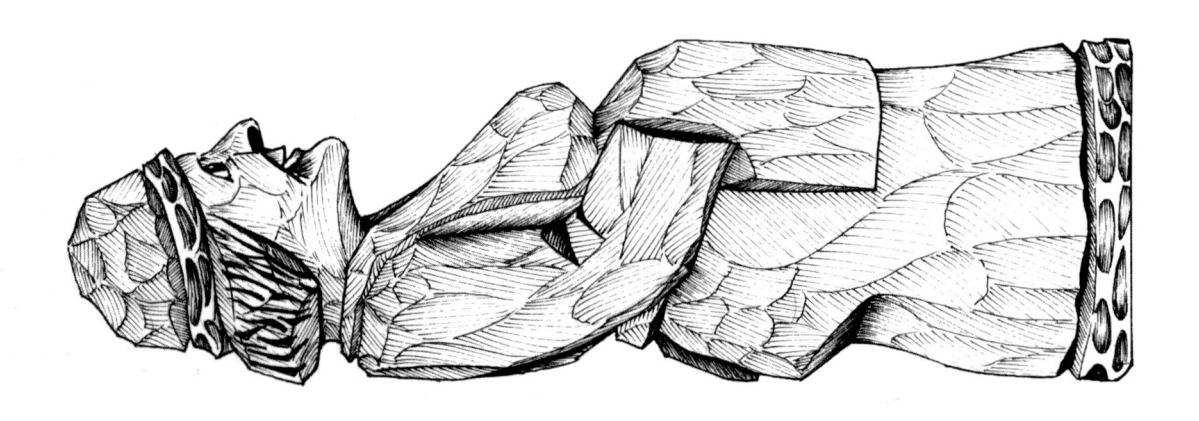

MRS. CLAUS

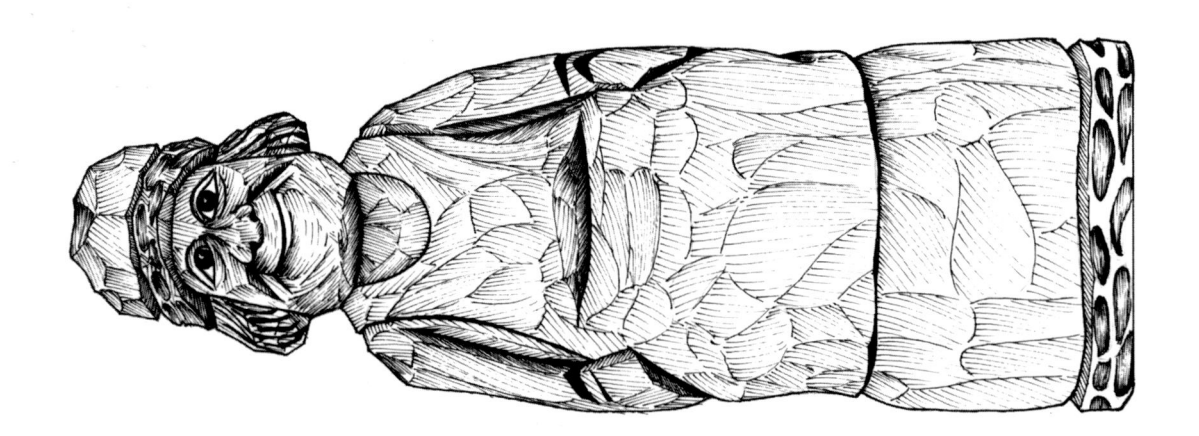

© Mike Shipley

Carving Snowmen and Santas

MRS. CLAUS

Here's a really fun piece to carve, and with her design, the possibilities are endless. Of course, she also makes a good couple with Mr. Claus. For a challenge, try carving something in her hands. (Height: 5 3/4")

Carving Snowmen and Santas 49 Patterns

MR. CLAUS

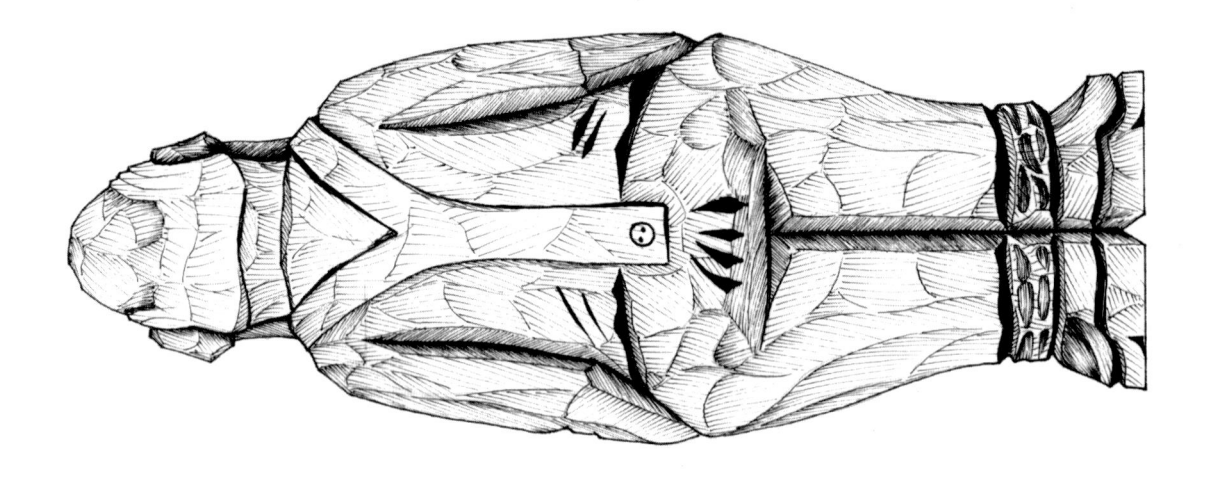

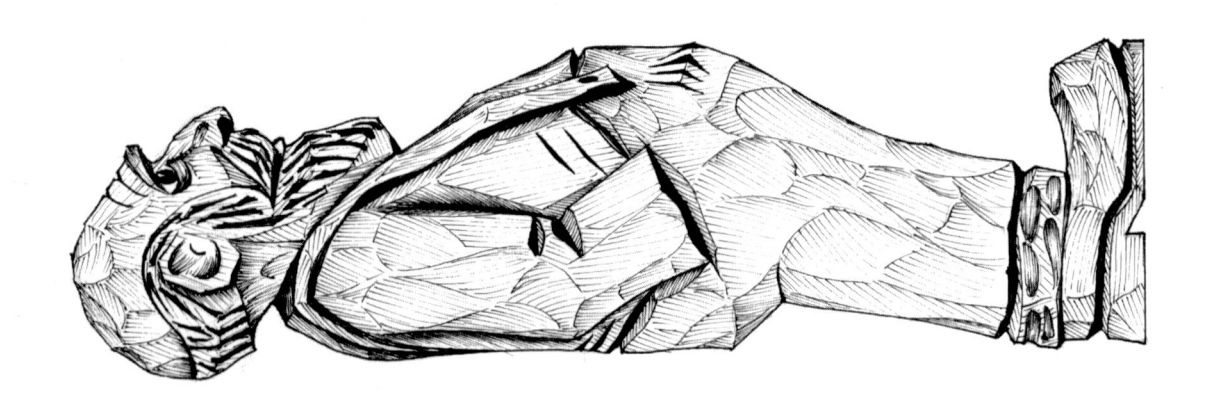

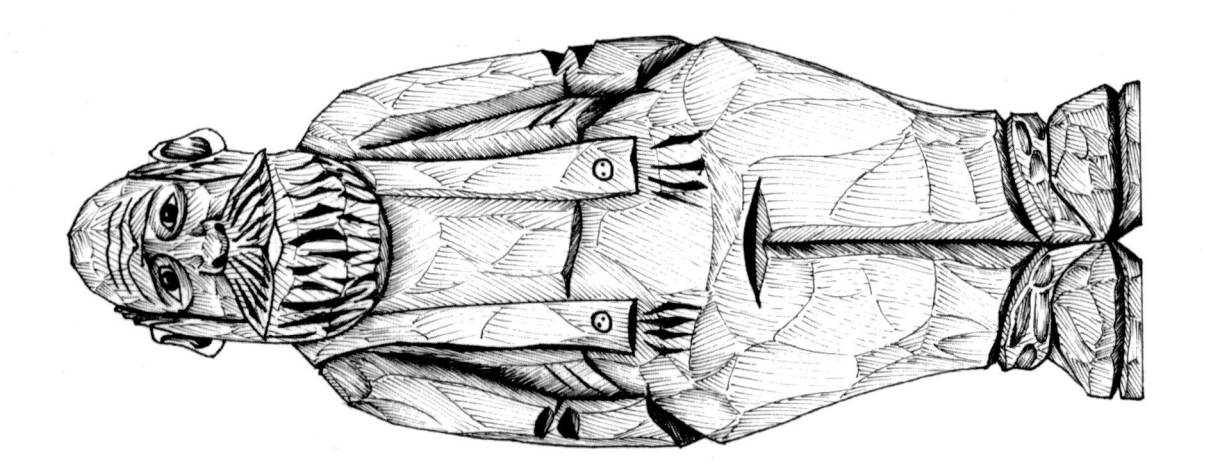

© Mike Shipley

Patterns • 50 • Carving Snowmen and Santas

MR. CLAUS

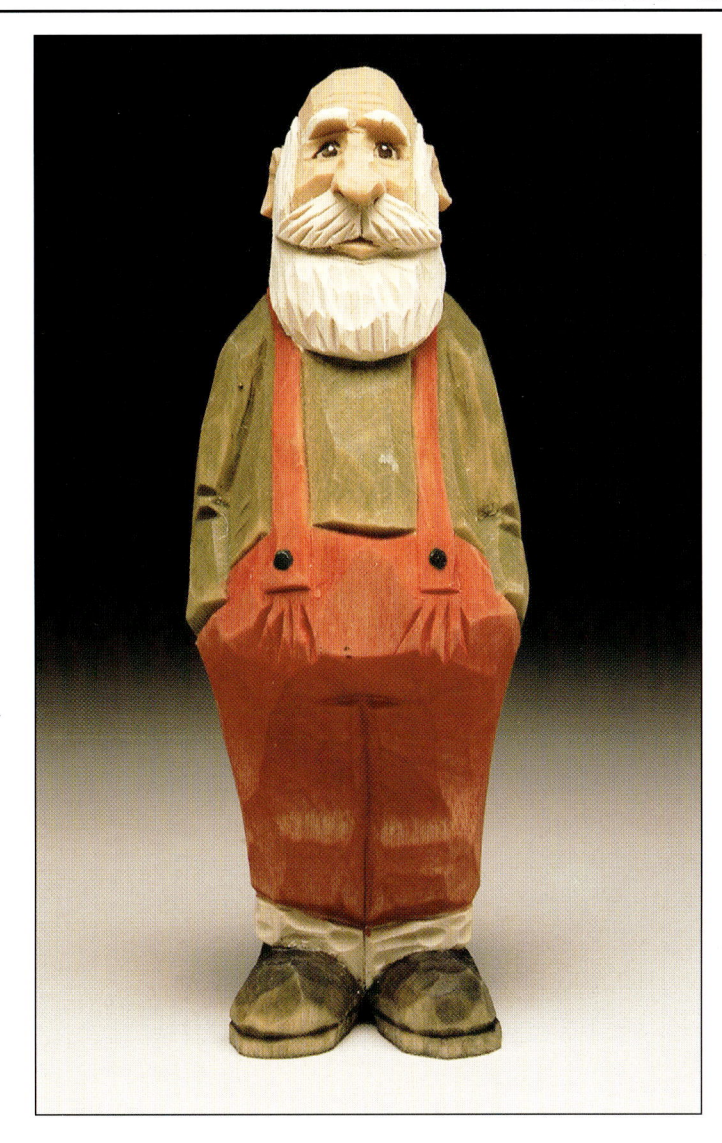

This is what Santa looks like when he gets home to relax after a long Christmas Eve. For a change, you might add a pipe in his mouth and dress him in a vest. Also try turning his head or tilting the head back. (Height: 5 3/4")

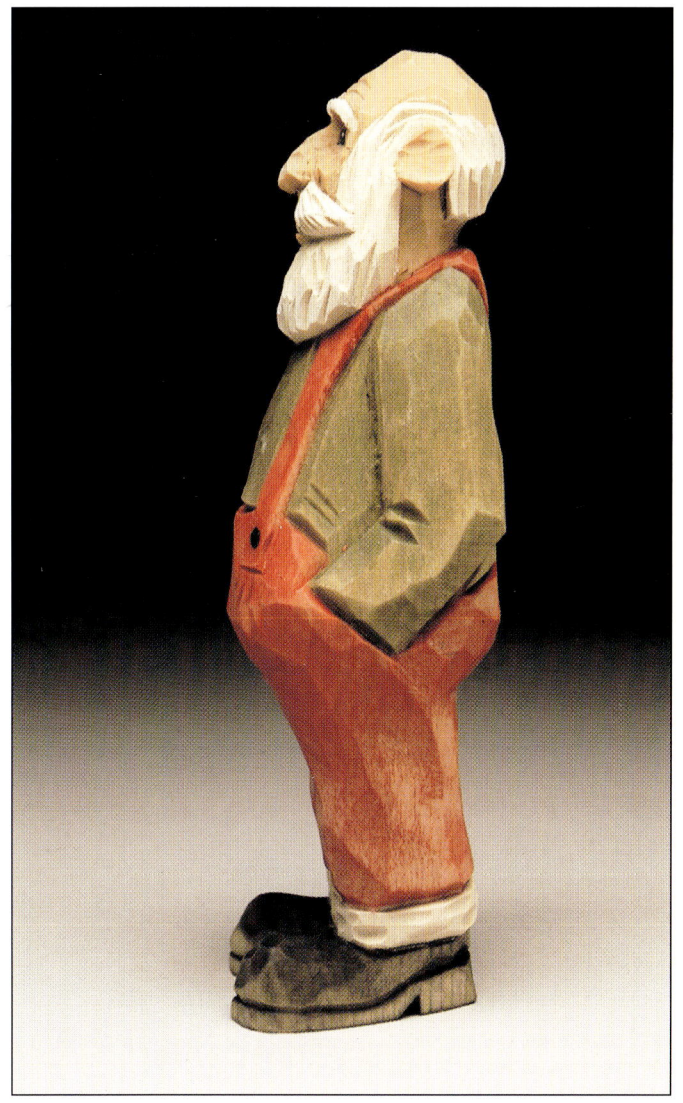

Carving Snowmen and Santas

Patterns

COWBOY SANTA

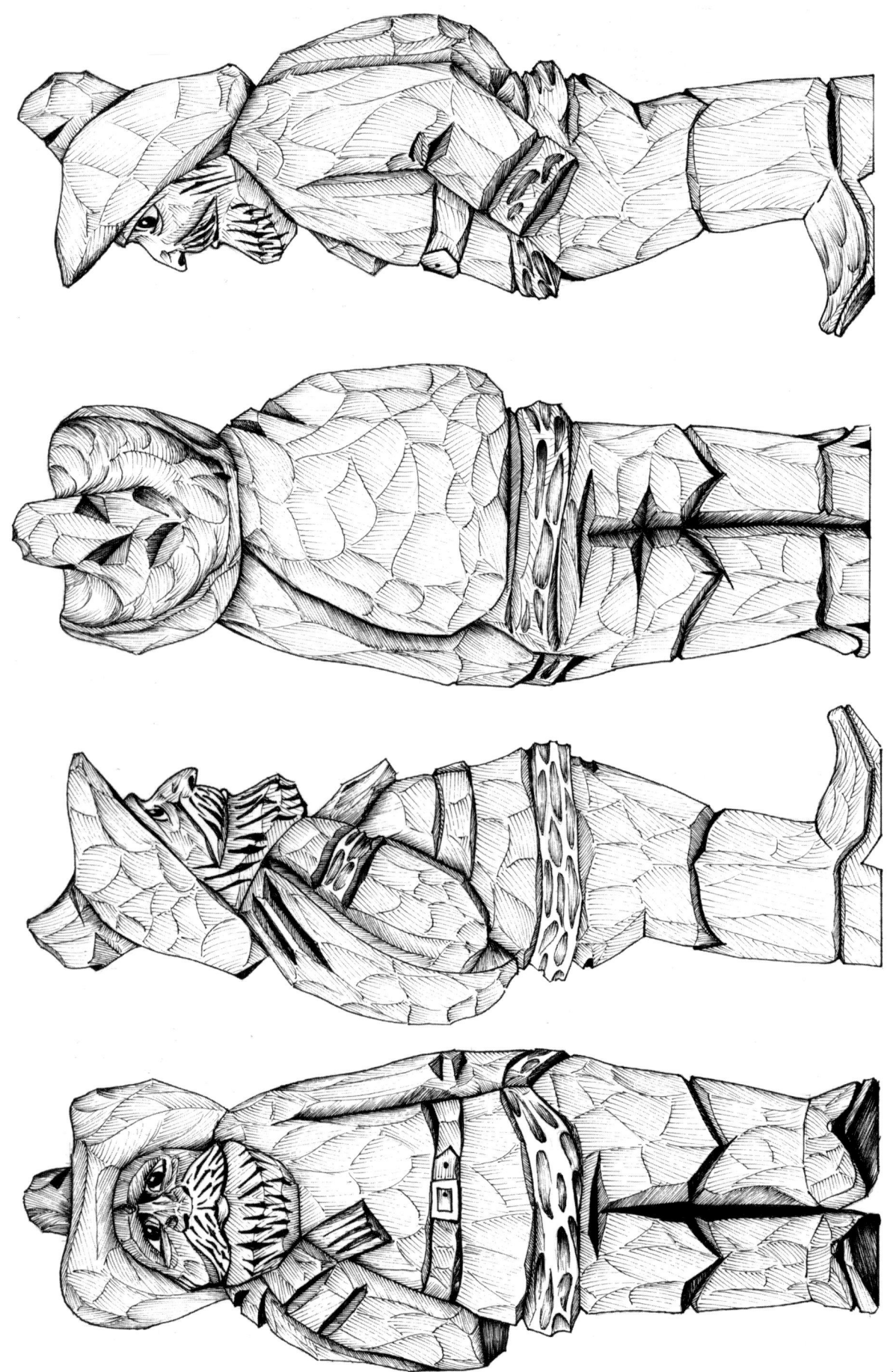

© Mike Shipley

Patterns 52 Carving Snowmen and Santas

COWBOY SANTA

Notice how this Santa resembles the Santa project in the step-by-step section? This is a good example of changing a pattern to have a totally different look. (Height: 6 1/4")

Carving Snowmen and Santas   Patterns

AFTERWORD

After working through the projects in this book, I'm sure you've found a few things that might be of use. As far as I know, I don't teach any new ground-breaking carving techniques. What I do try to teach are the basics and the constant refining of them. Carving improvement and success only comes from more carving. The more you carve, the more the basics become second nature. The two things I teach that I feel are the most important are to keep the piece simple and to keep it fun. Add a little confidence to that, and you might be surprised by the results. As someone once said, "In order to succeed we must first believe that we can."

If you have any questions or if you would like blanks for the projects in this book, contact me at the following address. I also offer woodcarving classes on a variety of topics.

Mike Shipley, woodcarving
Rt. 1 Box 4490
Dora, Mo 65637
417-284-3416

Fox Books Christmas Ideas

Fox Chapel Publishing Co. Inc.
1970 Broad Street • East Petersburg, PA 17520 • www.carvingworld.com

4 Easy Ways To Order!

1. Order by Phone:
1-800-457-9112
or 717-560-4703 (PA)
Customer Service Representatives are ready to assist you Monday - Friday 9:00 AM-5:00 PM (EST) Please have your Visa, Mastercard or Discover account number ready. Voice Mail is available 24 hours a day.

2. Order Toll Free by Fax:
1-888-369-2885
or 717-560-4702
Just write your order and credit card number with expiration date on a piece of paper & fax it to us anytime!

3. Order by Mail:
Send your order with check or money order with shipping (see rates below) included to:
Fox Books
1970 Broad Street, Dept. 129-5
East Petersburg, PA 17520
PLEASE DO NOT SEND CASH!

4. Order via Email/Online:
Email your order to:
sales@carvingworld.com
Order your favorite titles on-line at:
www.carvingworld.com

Don't Forget!
- Make all checks/money orders payable to: Fox Chapel Publishing.
- Please pay in US FUNDS only (available at any bank or post office)
- PA residents please add 6% sales tax.

Shipping
Most orders are shipped within 24 hours. If you need your books right away, please ask about overnight service when you call.

Order Subtotal	Shipping Cost USA	CANADA
$30 and under	$3	$5
$30.01 to $75	$4	$6
Over $75	$5	$8

FOREIGN orders will be billed the actual shipping cost.

Carving books make great gifts!

Creative Christmas Carving
By Tina Toney
Santas, santas, santas...and a couple of snowmen too! Within the pages of this book, you'll find 24 brilliant designs to decorate a Christmas tree and fill your home with the holiday spirit.
Patterns for each design are included, as well as a step-by-step demonstration with more than 50 photos to get you started.
Each ornament is carved from commercially available turnings or 3/8" thick basswood.
$14.95
64 pages, 8.5x11, soft cover.
ISBN# 1-56523-120-1

Santas & Snowmen: Carving for Christmas
By Tina Toney
Get into the spirit of the season with these 13 classics!
- Step-by-step demonstration
- Painting techniques
- Full color photos

$12.95
51 pages, 8.5x10.5, soft cover
ISBN# 1-56523-083-3

Making Collectible Santas and Christmas Ornaments in Wood
By Jim & Margie Maxwell
There is something inside for every holiday carver.
- 40 classic Christmas patterns
- Tools & materials list

$6.95
36 pages, 8.5x11, soft cover
ISBN# 1-56523-034-5

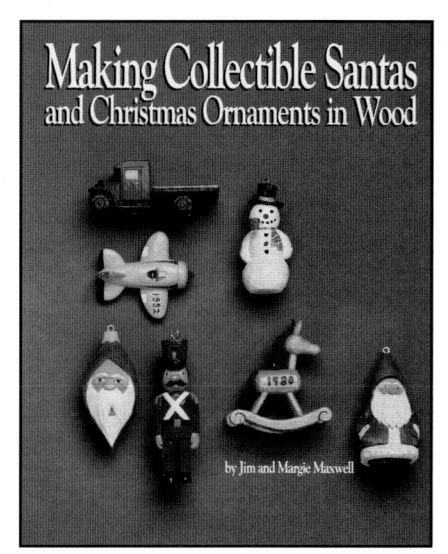

Santa Carving
With Myron Bowman
Give old St. Nick a facelift with these new ideas!
- 11 original patterns
- Step-by-step demonstration
- Carving and painting tips

$12.95
50 pages, 8.5x11, soft cover
ISBN# 1-56523-076-0

Fox Books Publisher's Picks

NEW!

Carving Crazy Critters
By Gary Batte

Bring a smile to even the most somber face with the characters in Gary Batte's new book. Ten clever projects are featured, complete with patterns, and finishing instructions. Sneak up on a down-and-out friend with "Al E. Gater," delight the woman in your life with "Buttercup, the Queen of Moo," give a hunter a laugh with "Flea-Bitis," make a child laugh with "Grumpy Gorilla," or move a slow-poke along with "Speedy the Tortoise."

You'll enjoy carving these delightful pieces as much as a friend or family member will enjoy receiving them.

$14.95
64 pages, 8.5x11, soft cover
ISBN# 1-56523-114-7

NEW!

Relief Carving - Patterns, Tips & Techniques
By William F. Judt

Join the ever-growing cadre of relief carvers with this complete introduction to relief carving. Author and artist Bill Judt shares tricks of the trade and personal insights gathered over his 13 years of relief carving.

Moving to the practical side of relief carving, he covers everything from choosing woods and buying chisels to laminating boards and stamping backgrounds. Included are a step-by-step demonstration and ready-to-use patterns to help you start your own relief-carving venture. Bill also includes advice for selling your work.

$19.95 *(Available in November 1999)*
120 pages, 8.5x11, soft cover
ISBN# 1-56523-124-4

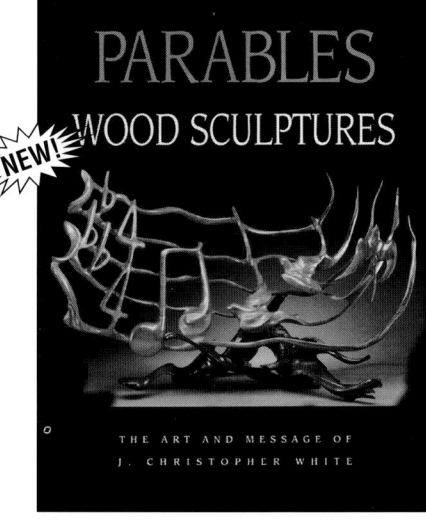

NEW!

Parables: Wood Sculptures
By J. Christopher White

We're excited about publishing this book! Chris White takes gnarled trees and roots and works within these natural forms to create stunningly beautiful works of art. These carved sculptures are sometimes realistic, sometimes stylized, but always highly evocative—even poetic and full of meaning.

The full color gallery photos and technical chapters appeal to carvers, sculptors and fine artists. The sheer beauty of each piece is accentuated with the artist's description of its creation and how it relates to his deep faith. This is an inspiring and interesting coffee table book.

$34.95 *(Available in November 1999)*
128 pages, 8.5x11, hard cover
ISBN# 11-56523-122-8

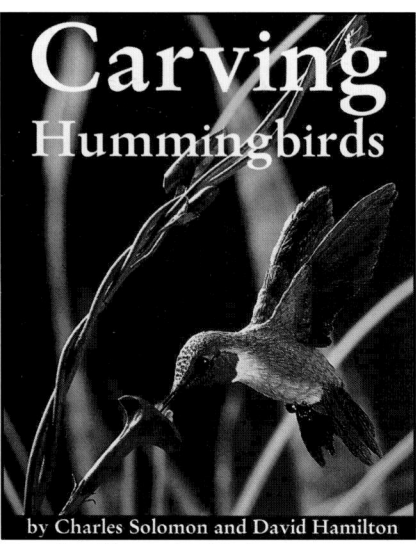

Carving Hummingbirds
By Charles Solomon & David Hamilton
2nd Revised Printing

If you have ever tried to carve one, you know why hummingbirds can be a carver's most exhilarating challenge!
- Anatomical illustrations that show wing position during hovering flight
- 2 step-by-step demonstrations
- More than 75 color photos
- Detailed instructions on creating a habitat

$19.95
62 pages, 8.5x11, soft cover
ISBN# 1-56523-064-7

Folk & Figure Wood Carving
By Ross Oar

Start your next figure carving using any of these traditional folk images.
- 17 detailed patterns
- Full color photos
- Adaptable to different skill levels

$14.95
52 pages, 8.5x11, soft cover
ISBN# 1-56523-105-8

Carving the Human Face - Capturing Character and Expression in Wood
By Jeff Phares

If you're having trouble creating life-like human fac[e] this is the book for you! World Champion carver Jeff Phares, well known for his lifelike busts and masks, reveals his techniques for creating masterful human portraits in wood.
- More than 350 instructional photographs to take you from a block of butternut to the finished facial mask of a Native American warrior.
- Diagrams explaining facial anatomy and how it relates to carving masks and busts.

Woodcarvers and sculptors alike will find new mate[ri]al and techniques inside this definitive, full-color guid[e]

$24.95
104 pages, 8.5x11, soft cover
ISBN# 1-56523-102-3

Fox Books Best Sellers

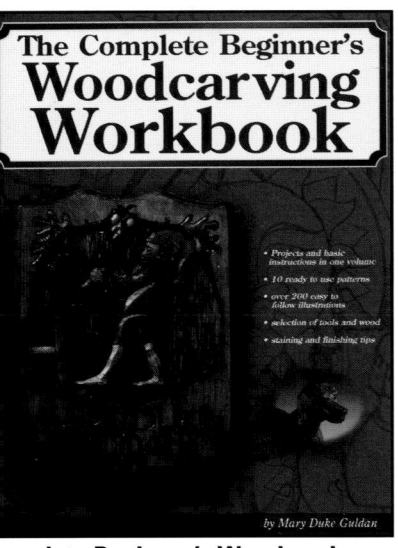

Complete Beginner's Woodcarving Workbook
By Mary Duke Guldan
There's something for everyone inside—relief carving, animals, faces & figures.
- Complete instructions on tool usage, sharpening, wood & tool selection
- Explicit step-by-step technique sections
- Special section about paints, stains & hardware.

$9.95
pages, 8.5x11, soft cover
ISBN# 1-56523-085-X

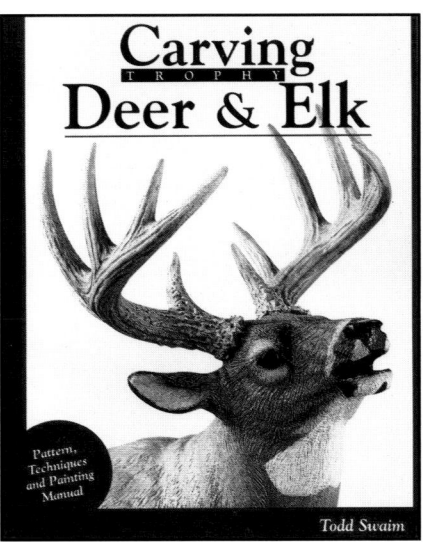

Carving Trophy Deer & Elk
By Todd Swaim
No one can capture the majesty of deer & elk like wildlife artist Todd Swaim.
- Complete step-by-step techniques shown in full color
- Beautiful gallery of finished examples
- Anatomy sketches, painting charts & hair tract illustrations

$19.95
74 pages, 8.5x11, soft cover
ISBN# 1-56523-089-2

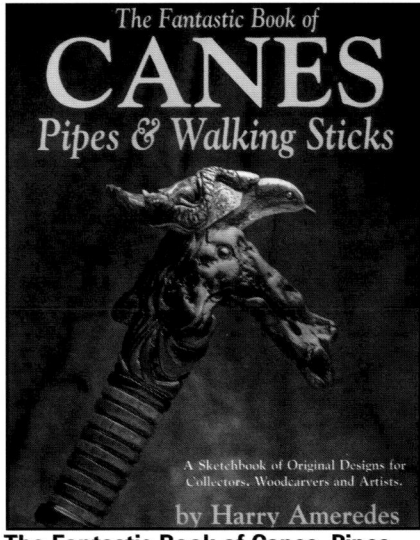

The Fantastic Book of Canes, Pipes and Walking Sticks
By Harry Ameredes
This sketchbook will keep you fascinated for hours!
- Original pen & ink design sketches
- Hundreds of ideas
- Highly recommended

$12.95
110 pages, 8x10, soft cover
ISBN# 1-56523-048-5

Carving Spoons
Shirley Adler
Spoons are fun, simple projects to develop your carving creativity & express yourself.
- 23 full size ready-to-use patterns
- Full color step-by-step instructions
- Features Welsh love spoons & Celtic knots

$14.95
pages, 8.5x11, soft cover
ISBN# 1-56523-092-2

Relief Carving Treasury
By William F. Judt
Through pictures & patterns, see what is possible for the carver working in relief.
- 16 gorgeous projects (intermediate)
- Full color photographs
- Detailed notes & technique tips

$14.95
74 pages, 8.5x11, soft cover
ISBN# 1-56523-097-3

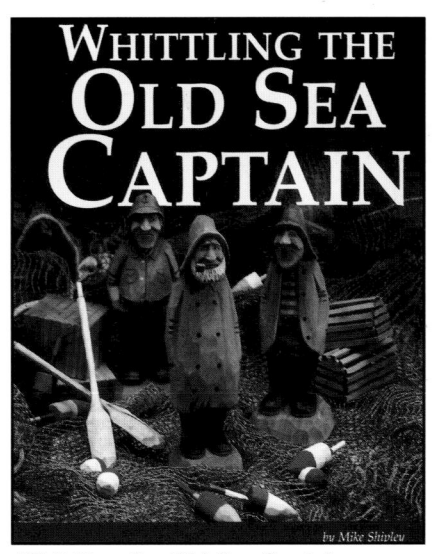

Whittling the Old Sea Captain
By Mike Shipley
Ahoy, there mate! Come aboard with carver Mike Shipley as he shows you how to carve a sea-worthy old captain and his crew.
- More than 100 step-by-step photos on carving, painting & staining
- Patterns for the Captain and his 1st & 2nd mates
- Information & more patterns for making buoys, lobster traps & wooden crates

$12.95
31 pages, 8.5x11, soft cover
ISBN# 1-56523-075-2

Fox Books Best Sellers

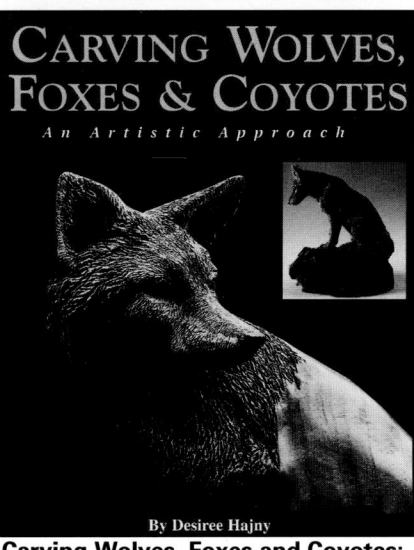

**Carving Wolves, Foxes and Coyotes:
An Artistic Approach**
By Desiree Hajny
Step-by-step instructions, along with artist notes and reference guides, were gathered to bring you this definitive guide to carving canines. The most recent addition to the Artistic Approach Series, Carving Wolves, Foxes and Coyotes includes more than 140 photographs detailing how to carve, burn and paint a wolf. Also included are natural history notes, anatomy sketches and reference photos for wolves, foxes and coyotes. Use the information to alter any one of the dozen patterns included in the book or combine details to design your own masterpiece.
$19.95
87 pages, 8.5x11, soft cover
ISBN# 1-56523-098-1

**Carving Small Animals:
An Artistic Approach**
By Desiree Hajny
Explicit color photos show how to carve, burn and paint small animals mammals. Clearly illustrated charts focus on hard-to-carve areas such as eyes, ears, noses and feet. Add realism to your work with the aid of color-coded anatomical charts and skeletal drawings. A step-by-step demonstration covers techniques that carvers can use on any small animal.
$14.95
53 pages, 8.5x11, soft cover.
ISBN# 1-56523-073-6

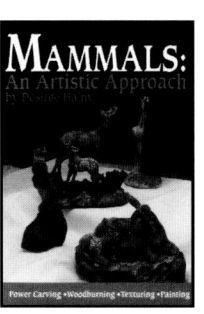

Mammals: An Artistic Approach
By Desiree Hajny
This classic book focuses on the playful otters, graceful deer and majestic bears. Through study sketches, reference photos and anatomy charts, Desiree gives you all the information you need to plan a beautiful carving. Burning techniques and a color section on painting covers Desiree's championship techniques are covered. Eighteen patterns are inside, including a skunk, ferret, ermine, elk, moose and a polar bear.
$19.95
154 pages, 8.5x11, soft cover
ISBN# 1-56523-036-1

**Big Cats: An Artistic Approach-
Carving Lions, Tigers & Jaguars**
By Desiree Hajny
Detailed notes and anatomy charts will give you all the background to these beautiful animals. Charts illustrate techniques for legs, feet, eyes, ears, noses and mouths. Learn to create the illusion of fur.
$14.95
51 pages, 8.5x11, soft cover
ISBN# 1-56523-071-X

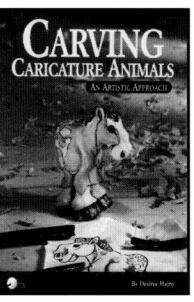

**Carving Caricature Animals:
An Artistic Approach**
By Desiree Hajny
Animal caricatures guaranteed to make you smile! Clearly written text and carefully drawn illustrations teach you how to focus in on the best features to caricature on any animal. Use the full-page charts to easily carve every feature, from eyes and ears to tail and feet. Eight ready-to-use patterns of the most popular projects are included.
$14.95
48 pages, 8.5x11, soft cover
ISBN# 1-56523-074-4

Wood Carving ILLUSTRATED

Subscribe Today!

"Every Carver's How-To Magazine"

It's like having a master carver at your side!

Future Issues will feature:

- Burl Wood
- Fish Gallery
- Building Your Own Drying Kiln
- Carving Pipes
- Chip Carved Quilt
- Carving Chess Sets
- Raptors

Discover the carving secrets of the masters and apply them to your work!

Make your carvings come alive with our painting and finishing tips!

Special projects just for beginning carvers!

Our easy-to-follow instructions and color photos guide you from a block of wood to the finished piece.

FREE
with a 2-year subscription!
Power Carving Manual
2nd volume
a $9.95 Value!
120 pages in full color

Don't miss another issue! Return this form today.

2 Years
- [ ] $39.90 *USA*
- [ ] $45.00 *Canada (US Funds only)*
- [ ] $55.90 *Foreign (US Funds only)*

1 Year
- [ ] $19.95 *USA*
- [ ] $22.50 *Canada (US Funds only)*
- [ ] $27.95 *Foreign (US Funds only)*

Please allow 4-6 weeks for delivery of your first issue.

Method of Payment
- [ ] Check/Money Order *(US Funds only)*
- [ ] Visa, MC or Discover

Name on card _____ Exp. date _____

Card number _____

NAME _____
ADDRESS _____
CITY _____ STATE/PROV _____
ZIP/PC _____
PHONE _____
E-MAIL _____

Send your completed order form to: Wood Carving Illustrated, 1970 Broad Street N., East Petersburg, PA 17520

129-5